So, You Want To Be A Doctoral Learner Huh?
ARE YOU NUTS?!

A short story of my difficult journey

as an online doctoral learner, and

some tips to help you succeed

By

Dr. L. A. Davis

Copyright © 2018 by Dr. L. A. Davis
Published 2018 by Doctrine101 Press
New Castle, DE

All rights for this publication reserved. No part of this book may be reproduced, stored in a retrieval system, or transmitted in any form or by any means to include electronic, mechanical, digital, photocopy, recording, or by any other means. Excerpts may be used in brief quotations in printed reviews without prior permission of the publisher or author. All pictures are the property of the author and are copyright protected.

Special Thanks: Mr. Lester Harvey at grafixvi@gmail.com
Cover Graphic: Nazriel0707 and elite_cover on Instagram
Section Graphics: rainbow_toons and Nazriel0707 on Instagram
Back Cover Photo: Photo Depot
Diploma Graphics: Created in Microsoft Word
Tam and Robe Graphics: Free Graphics

Library of Congress Cataloging-in-Publication Data
Davis, L. A.

ISBN: 978-1-64254-550-0

So, You Want To Be A Doctoral Learner Huh? ARE YOU NUTS?!/Dr. L. A. Davis

    p. cm.

1. Education and Teaching   2. Higher Education

0 1 2 3 4 5 6 7 8 9

Printed in the United States of America

DEDICATION

I dedicate this book to the thousands of novice researchers who are so filled with love for others that they chose to embrace their nutty side by achieving their Doctor of Education (Ed. D) or Doctor of Philosophy (Ph.D.).

FOREWORD
By Dr. Keith Adams

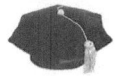

The completion of the doctoral degree is an individual challenging task, yet a collective one. The completion of a doctoral degree is an individual task because it entails one passion about a topic that provides the intrinsic motivation which drives the dissertation bus. The completion of a doctoral degree is a collective task because of the amount of external support and motivation that is needed to sustain everyone throughout their doctoral journey. The level of sacrifice and commitment needed is unparalleled to any other journey along your path in life. Throughout the doctoral journey, you will meet people who will have a profound influence on you. For me, Dr. Davis was one of the most influential people during my doctoral journey.

When I met Dr. Davis, we both experienced struggles through the doctoral process. During our initial meeting, we shared parts of our journey and discovered we shared a passion for helping people. I learned throughout my doctoral process that it takes a team effort to complete this journey. Dr. Davis is the type of person who you want on your team because she is a fierce competitor, a key ally, a great listener, and is available to assist in any way she can. Her book serves as a roadmap for doctoral learners at every stage.

Everyone's doctoral journey is different; however, all doctoral students will go through challenging times. Developing an action plan, along with using a variety of resources, can help doctoral learners complete their journey. Dr. Davis has provided an outstanding resource for the doctoral learner to assist them in navigating this challenging process. The use of this book along with other resources can have a positive effect on the learner's progress as they navigate through the various stages of the doctoral journey. In conclusion, I want to wish you the best of luck with your doctoral journey. All the Best.

TABLE OF CONTENTS

DEDICATION..iii
FOREWORD..v
Introduction..1
In the Beginning...5
The Difference Between A Ph.D. and an Ed. D..........................9
The Lingo of a Doctoral Learner...13
My First Residency..15
Choosing A Topic..20
Research Tips...25
Mind, Body, Spirit...35
No Short Cuts..45
Dissertation Committee...47
My Second Residency..58
Really Dark Days...62
When Murphy's Law and Data Collection Shake Hands......78
Data Analysis...87
Death of My Dearest Cohort...91
The Finish Line...95
Living In The Moment...101
Going Home...105
Reflections..108
Conclusion...113
Research Assignments..119
Website Resources..122
Visualization Graphics...123
INDEX..127
ABOUT THE AUTHOR...129

Introduction

In 2015, I thought about writing a book. January 31, 2016, I started writing it. I could not finish until 2018 -- the year I would complete my doctoral journey. I came up with the idea because of a negative experience I had with a committee member who I felt did not have my best interest in mind. He made my journey as difficult as possible, and the university refused to help.

I like speaking in detailed layman terms that are not boring. I do not walk around demanding everyone call me Dr. Davis or speak with words that make me appear pompous. I like to walk around my home in workout clothes, oversized sweat suits, slippers, and getting involved in the occasional daredevil antics whenever I get the chance.

Authoring this book was a lot of fun. I did not have to use any in-text citations or references, and I had no due dates to stress over. I tried not to use words that would make you have to hold a thesaurus in one hand and a dictionary in the other, but you can do so if you feel the need.

I authored this book in a manner as if someone is talking to a friend so you can relax and focus on what I am saying. There is no need to ask, let us get this out of the way right now. Your journey will be hard.

Introduction

It will be unlike anything you have ever experienced, and you will shed tears.

While you go through your doctoral or Ph.D. journey, you will need to dress professionally, speak scholarly, and walk with confidence. While you read this book, you can dress and speak any way you choose.

My intent is not to beat up on the university. I only want to share my personal experience and show you how I came out on top. In doing so, my desire is this information might be of help to you. I did not identify the university or personnel because I wanted to protect the innocent, and the guilty.

Additionally, I am not bashing online schooling. Online educational programs of study allow adults to earn an income while they obtain a terminal degree. I attended an online university while earning my master's degree and loved every bit of it. Unfortunately, many online institutions are more concerned with revenue than the needs of the learner. At least in my experience, this was the case.

These words are from my personal experience and perspective, no one else's. When people I knew said to me, "I am going to get my Ph.D.," I looked at them and asked, "Are you crazy?" I am not making light of mental illness. I knew what they were about to get into and to experience. To me, only a "crazy" person would do this to themselves.

There were numerous times I went through terrible bouts of depression and felt I had to be "nuts" to be doing this. I felt as if I was in a dream state for half of my journey, hence the caricatures shown in the various stages of this book. You might be feeling the same way too, but those feelings have a place in your journey and will be forever with you.

Although every university has its own program, all doctoral learners go through the same emotions at some point in their journey. There will be moments of excitement, fear, despair, anger, confusion, depression, worry, anxiety, and an abundant amount of loneliness.

Do your best to enjoy your journey and remember it is neither worth your physical or mental health, the loss of your family, nor the loss of your life. You will either be a doctor, or you will need one. In some cases, it might be both; but once you are done, you will never have to do it again.

Since being in an advanced degree program does not allow much time or desire to read, I only shared a snippet of my experience. There are five and a half years stuffed between these covers. If you look at it that way, the number of pages will not seem too bad.

Hints, tips, and techniques are presented throughout this book in no specific order. Grab a pen, notebook, or use the last pages I provided at the end to take notes. I hope this information helps you before, during or after choosing a Doctor of Education (Ed.D.) or Doctor of Philosophy (Ph.D.) program.

Doctoral and Ph.D. journeys are difficult. Some professors seem to make it their mission to make it more difficult than it needs to be. It would be impossible for me to write every incident; therefore, I focused on pivotal events which made me quit driving my bus.

The first two years of my doctoral program were stressful and at the same time a wonderful experience. I had to think, write, and learn differently, and in a new way. Everything I learned in my courses proved later to be beneficial information. Research papers excited me to write and weekly class postings created enlightening conversations.

Many of you reading this book will cut your journey short. There is an extremely high attrition rate for doctoral learners. This might not sound encouraging to you, but please understand it is the nature of the beast. You will go through bouts of depression and experience an overwhelming feeling of failure. This is normal, but always remember you will still be awesome. Come and take a ride with me as I sit back, buckle up, fix my mirrors, and enjoy the view as I drive my bus.

Introduction

BEFORE MY DOCTORAL STUDIES

In the Beginning

Before I started my doctoral journey, I felt free as a bird and wished myself the best of luck and best wishes. It excited me to explore a Ph.D. program; life was good. Reality smacked me in my face when I discovered I had no idea what I was doing.

You decided to work toward your Ph.D. or Ed.D. Which one suits you and why? Did you choose one of these programs because you wanted to brag about having an advanced degree? Did you choose it because you wanted to have the letters after your name? Or, was it because you liked the way Dr. sounded before your name? If any of these are the case, I am asking you to stop right now and forget about it. You are wasting your time and money.

Two years after graduating with a master's degree in Criminal Justice with an emphasis in Law, I decided to earn my Ph.D. I thought about it after having a conversation with a woman I met while sitting under a dryer in a hair salon at 6 a.m. Yes, I said six in the morning. I wanted to go to law school, but the LSAT ate me alive, my state did not allow law students to work during the first year and I needed the income to support my family. After my less than stellar performance on my LSAT, I considered it a divine intervention. I invested money and time in preparation for the exam with poor results. My dissertation at the time of this writing was being read as far as the continent of Africa. A law degree could not do that.

There was not a university which offered a Ph.D. program close to my home which led me to investigate online institutions. Ultimately, I chose a school a friend attended at the time and failed to perform due diligence to vet it. After the first week of class, I decided to find another institution because in the twelve weeks I attended, I never heard one word from anyone about their Ph.D. program as they only spoke of the university. After looking at different universities, I scoffed at some names because they seemed sketchy to me. I checked the cost of their programs, the length of the programs and credit hours needed to complete the degree. I also asked if they had only online programs or if they had brick and mortar facilities.

I requested enrollment information from a brick and mortar university with an online extension program. After ignoring the incessant phone calls for a week from this university, I decided to return the call and have a long discussion with an enrollment advisor. I asked the university's location, their core values, the program cost, and the length of their doctoral program.

When the advisor answered my questions, I decided to give it a go after he provided me information on other programs and universities so I could compare them. I wonder now if that was a red flag, or did this a person try to convince me the program he represented was the best choice? After checking other programs, I decided to enroll in this university which will remain nameless.

I now faced the decision of which Ph.D. program to choose. When I looked at the statistics courses I had to complete for a Ph.D., my heart started to pound. I am old enough to know when I am getting ready to shoot myself in the foot. I hate pain and avoid it like the plague. I know to entertain any of the Ph.D. programs is like setting myself up for difficulties, or failure. To explain, I am going to share short stories from when I was a youngster.

In junior high school on my tiny island home, I had an American math teacher. I loved this math teacher because he had an incredible amount of humor and energy. You knew when you attended his class, you were going to have fun.

One day when everyone was settled into their seats, this teacher decided to pull out his grade book and read every grade of every student in the class. I knew it was not going to end well for me. When he got to my name, he started reading my grades. His voice was normal. As he continued to read, his voice got deeper, and deeper to show that my grade was going lower and lower. When he got to the end, his voice could not go any deeper. The entire class was in stitches. It embarrassed me, but at the same time, it was funny. After all these years, I am unable to think or write about it without laughing. Now on to my high school experience.

I attended high school in Brooklyn. My high school had a co-op program. The program allowed me to go to school for one week and work the next week to get experience in the workforce. One day while at my job, my algebra teacher gave the class a test. I knew the following week I would have to take it. I went to class on Monday. As the teacher began the lesson, I raised my hand to get his attention. He looked me in the face, waved his hands, and told me not to worry about the test. My average in the class was an F. I guess he thought it would be a waste of time. No one knew I had to take the test, but I was still embarrassed. I was also annoyed that I wasted my entire week worrying about it. After that class my counselor placed me in a record-keeping class where I excelled.

Although I managed to pass math classes by the skin of my teeth, I avoided them as much as possible. After teleporting from those areas of my memory, I reached out to my enrollment advisor.

I told him I wished there was a way I could come and visit the university to see what it looked like, and what it had to offer.

He informed me the university had a new program that allowed potential learners to fly in for a day. I could meet the staff and tour the campus. He scheduled a trip, but due to inclement weather in another city, my flight was canceled. Everything had to be rescheduled. The second trip went on without a hitch. Was this delay in my flight a second red flag?

While in flight to visit the university, I met two people who like me were going to the day visit, but who planned to enroll in different programs if all went according to their liking. We landed after a couple of hours. The university supplied car service for us. That was a new experience, and we loved it. When we arrived at the campus, everyone met in a reception area where they gave us a light breakfast.

Faculty, staff, and department heads attended to answer questions and a tour of this beautiful campus followed. I asked myself, "How in the world do students focus on attending classes surrounded by this beautiful place?" It looked like an oasis in the middle of a desert. After the tour, we separated into groups by degree levels.

We went to a room to meet, greet, and ask questions. I am naturally inquisitive. I asked how long breaks were between classes. The professor told me there were no breaks between them. When I asked her why, she said, "Because they want you to get out in three years." After our meeting, we went to another building to have lunch.

The woman I asked about the break sat at my table. I told her my concerns about the statistics classes because I was poor at math. She suggested I look at the Ed.D. programs because I had to be able to input the information into the program. I had no idea what program or information she was talking about, but she was moving her fingers to simulate typing while she talked.

After lunch, a short speech from the head of the university followed. From there they took me to a long table to learn about my financial aid opportunities. It was a fast-paced day that started early in the morning and ended when I got home late that night.

The next day I called my enrollment advisor and told him I was not sure this educational step was for me. I was extremely poor at math and I felt the number of statistics courses required for the program would be too difficult. The only other program included the Ed.D. program, and I would not be able to publish in research journals which was what I wanted to do.

He told me I was mistaken; I could publish in journals with an Ed.D. I had never heard of a Doctor of Education degree before. I took the time to investigate that program. Great news! I only had to take one Statistics course. The available Ed.D. program suited me and my desires more than the Ph.D. program; so, in 2012, I became an official Ed. D. learner.

The Difference Between A Ph.D. and an Ed.D.

Many of you might be enrolled in a program while others may have only a general idea and appreciation about a Ph.D. or an Ed.D. degree. For now, I am speaking to the novice researcher who like me, may not be aware of a degree called Doctor of Education.

A Doctor of Philosophy (Ph.D.) is an ingenious person whose study is heavily research-based and a Doctor of Education (D.Ed. or Ed.D.) is an ingenious person whose study is heavily curriculum-based; a practitioner.

I earned my Doctor of Education in leadership. For two years I took leadership courses along with a few research courses. Institutions may have a different program set up. Do your research before choosing one and do it diligently. Each degree has the benefit of producing a dissertation consisting of five chapters.

You will be able to teach at the university level, and you will have opportunities that other degree levels will not afford you. You will conduct your own research and you will add to the body of literature (research) by "riding the coattails" of someone before you. Both degrees will give you the title of doctor.

One day, someone may "ride your coattails" by adding to your dissertation. Do your research to see which degree is best for you. Now that you have a brief idea of the difference between both degrees, we can move on to fun things.

I had to choose the program where I would spend the next three years showing the world how smart I thought I was to academia. I had a professor who told me early in my program that earning a doctorate had nothing to do with being smart. It had to do with persistence, and this is a fact. Let me repeat. Persistence!

During the recruitment stage to enroll in the university, the advisor told me the program took three years to complete, and he assured and reassured me the timeframe and he provided me with the breakdown. In the end, I received new information that was not provided in the beginning. By the time I figured it out, it was too late to turn back.

I gave myself a short-term goal of five years to complete my Ed.D. program to give myself a break between courses if I needed one. The first course oriented me to the university and to the academic world to earn my degree. The course also described how my dissertation was woven 'naturally' into the courses. Although this was a part of the marketing, I found it to be untrue.

The first strange word I learned was an "empirical" article. It is the proper term for the commonly known word "peer reviewed." Throughout my years of academia, I had never heard this term. Once you become a doctoral learner, you will learn a lot of unfamiliar and several extremely large academic terms which by all accounts proved as a double-edged sword for me. Keep reading, I explained it later in this book.

After becoming a doctoral learner, I was unable to look at things the same. If someone showed me two "identical" cups, my mind could not accept these cups as "identical." I had to ask, "How do you know they are identical? What instruments did you use to measure this? What color are the cups? What kind of paint did they use? How much paint did they use? What kind of brushes did they use? Did they have the same amount of bristles? Were the bristles made of the same material? Did the cups weigh the same? What kind of scale did you use? When was the scale last calibrated? What did you use to calibrate the scale?" Yes, it will happen to you too.

One misconception of new learners is that they will conduct a study to prove something. A dissertation is not written to prove anything. You are going to take someone else's research and add to it by conducting your own research. You will answer their questions as you create some of your own. You will share your findings so that your topic becomes relevant to the body of literature. Your study will allow the research you used to remain current and will make you an expert in your field.

During my doctoral studies, the university's policy allowed me to take only one course at a time. One course was considered full-time. I could not understand why each course was only three credit hours, and I did not think enough to ask. I needed sixty credits to get to the start of my dissertation part of the program. In my Master degree program, I needed fifty-five credit hours to earn my degree, and I earned five credits in each course.

I quickly understood their one course at a time reasoning as the law of the land and why the courses were only three credits once embedded into the course work. Each course required numerous hours of research and writing. On the flip side, for the university's profit margin, three credit hours per course brought in revenue. I thought if I earned five credit hours in a master's program, it would be the same for my doctorate. It was a big oversight on my part in terms of my finances and time to complete the program.

Also, during each three-credit course I filtered through many empirical articles a week required to find two or three to compare and contrast to enhance a specific skill called synthesizing; a skill all learners must acquire and be proficient at it to be successful. One thing I appreciated about reading empirical articles was finding the kinds of writing style I liked and disliked.

A doctoral or Ph.D. learner must write academically. Many of these scholarly articles were unreadable or difficult to understand for me. Nothing frustrated me more than having to pull out a dictionary and a thesaurus while combing the studies. I could not understand what many of the researchers tried to say or what their research contained.

One of my professors told me I had "A different way of writing." I am not ashamed of this fact. It is what makes me unique. I wanted my writing to be available to anyone who is willing to pick up my work whether they are blind or sighted. A blind person may not be able to read, but they can listen, and I wanted my work to include everyone, so they could understand it. More than that, I wanted whoever picked up my work to be able to walk away with an understanding of what I wrote. What is the sense of writing something others cannot read or understand?

When you become a doctoral or Ph.D. learner, you will find the best way to deliver your message. If you are the type of writer who uses large words that a reader must pick up a dictionary or thesaurus; be proud of it – be you.

In my program, I needed two residencies. During my first year, everything went well, and I was on schedule to attend my first one. Residency provided online learners with the opportunity to have one-on-one class time with professors, guidance on choosing my topic of research, and to align my dissertation outline. It also helped me in other skill areas in which I deemed a weakness to better equip myself for the remainder of my program. Residency required long hours and diligent work.

In my first residency, I discovered that earning a doctorate or Ph.D. had its own language. I call this language, the doctoral lingo.

The Lingo of a Doctoral Learner

In the doctoral or the Ph.D. world, the language is different. It can make for a lonely process when you know what you are talking about but no one else around you has a clue. It is worse when you think you know what you are talking about, but you really do not, and neither does anyone else.

I broke the dissertation down into parts like a body. The body of the dissertation is as follows. I referred to the first stage as the skeleton. The second stage as the nerves. The third stage as the muscles and inner organs. The fourth stage as the skin, the outer covering which holds the body of my literature (dissertation) together. This is how I reconciled this process in my mind. You may find another way to reconcile your stages. Choose whatever makes it easier for you to understand.

Here are some words you might see in a dissertation. Data analysis, literature review, theoretical foundation, conceptual framework, problem statement, hypothesis, variables, G*power, methodology, design, purpose statement, and phenomenological. How many of these terms do you understand? Do you think if you asked a friend or loved one to help you, they would understand what you are asking? Would they know what to do?

This is some of the lingo a doctoral or Ph.D. learner must become familiar with and the cause for much loneliness. This is what I meant earlier when I said that having this lingo is a double-edged sword. You are going to know a lot of fancy words that your friends and family will not understand. They will not be able to help you.

If you go to anyone who does not have one of these degrees or go to anyone who is not in a doctoral or Ph.D. program, they will likely shrug their shoulders. They will look at you like you are speaking another language. To them, you will be.

Choosing your methodology and design can cause a lot of frustration. You will have to decide if your study will be a qualitative methodology, a quantitative methodology, or a mixed methods methodology. You may decide which methodology you want to use before you choose your topic.

I caution you to pay attention to your gap or need statement, your topic, your research questions, your problem statement, and your purpose statements before you choose your methodology. Let them guide your methodology and design. I witnessed a few of my cohorts choose their methodology before their topic. When they were halfway into their process and made it to their dissertation part of the program, they had to change their study because the topic and research questions were not aligned with the methodology.

When you decide on your methodology, you will have to make sure you choose the right design, instruments, and data analysis. A great dissertation committee will do their best to make sure your study is right; some will not. It is your responsibility as a learner and researcher to choose the outcome of your research. You must understand what you are doing, and you must know how each work together. If not, it will be like putting gasoline in your bus when it runs on diesel.

My First Residency

I started the process of attending my first residency by choosing the week I wanted to attend and what day I needed to travel. The university chose the venue. All I had to do was make my room reservation, reserve an airline ticket, pay for residency, and check in. Unfortunately, I went to residency in August. I decided to take my children so they could do the vacay sway and see a new state before they headed back to a new school year.

This city where my residency would occur happened to be one of the most beautiful cities I had ever visited. It not only had some of the nicest people you would ever want to meet but also it was also the hottest place I had ever experienced. Thousands of miles from my tiny island home and hundreds of miles from the state I resided, I was not prepared for the onslaught of heat I experienced in this city located in the southwest. I arrived a day early. To think of what I would have had to deal with if I waited until the morning of residency made my head hurt and spin.

After checking in and settling into our room, I took my children to eat. All I wanted to do was drink, so I ordered a large-frosty-glass of lemonade. After lunch, we retreated to our room to rest. Our lodging was a small-cozy suite which smelled of old-rancid cigarettes.

My First Residency

To a non-smoker like myself, it nauseated me. I thought I could deal with the odor, but each time I walked into the room, it gave me a brand-new whiff experience of rancid. I considered requesting another room, but I was too tired to entertain the idea. What sealed the deal to move included me trying to find my way around the maze of the place. I got lost every time I left the room.

I called the front desk and asked if it was possible for me to relocate to the main building. They gave me the okay, but I could not move until the next day. After class the next day, someone from the staff was kind enough to drive us to our new room.

The room smelled better, and it was closer to the soothing sounds of a water fountain. It also was in the front of the venue and across the street from the classrooms. All I had to do now was walk around the corner and catch the elevator or walk down one flight of stairs. I could not get lost; I was in heaven.

Although there was a pool at their disposal and the constant humming of gigantic water fountains at every earshot, my children dared not go outside until after 5 p.m. There was no curfew, so they could come and go as they pleased. There was a beautiful water park, restaurants, spa, and gym and I gave them money every day before I went to class.

Instead of going to the restaurant on the premises, they chose room service. In all the years I worked, I never experienced room service. I encouraged them to go out and experience the venue, but they wanted nothing to do with the heat.

The first day of residency the food was nice, and it was served on glass plates and with real silverware.

After that day… well… I was still grateful. Many of the new learners were nervous. We did not have our required assignment completed. One professor informed the class she knew we would not have our assignments done because we did not know what many of the terms meant and she knew it. There was no reason for us to be nervous. If I had to do it again, I would have tried harder to find the answers to the assignment.

I met wonderful people from all over the country and was introduced to the topics other learners had chosen. It amazed me to see what the myriad of brilliant human minds brought forth for their topics. Not everyone at residency had their topic chosen, but everyone in our class managed to create ours. One learner had her entire assignment completed. Her mother graduated from the same program and took advantage of that as she knew what to do.

During your coursework, other learners may appear smarter and more put together than yourself. I caution you to stay in your lane, do not compare yourself to others, and continue to drive your bus. Someone may seem like they know it all, but that does not mean they are smarter, they will finish before you, or for that matter if they will graduate. I met other learners who started their program with me and got ahead when I took a short break. Some never completed their program and dropped out.

When I got in touch with them after an extended period, I had passed them in our program. I know learners who started in 2012 who are still struggling to get through it in 2018. Today I am Dr. Davis, but many of my cohort members are all but dissertation (ABD) with no desire to finish. Keep your eyes on the road and drive your bus.

Each day the classrooms were cold. Soaking up the coolness of the freezing rooms did not protect me from the vengeance waiting outside. In the state where I live you bake from the outside in, and you sweat due to humidity. In this city, I felt like I was baking from the inside out.

Several years ago, a coworker and I were in the break room. One thing I disliked about a workplace microwave oven is the inability of others to be considerate enough to clean it. On this day, I was especially annoyed to open the oven door and see ants crawling around inside. My coworker told me you can microwave ants, and nothing would happen to them. I did not believe him, so to prove it he told me to start the microwave oven. I closed the door and turned it on for sixty seconds. When I opened the door, the ants were unbothered as they continued to scavenge for morsels of food.

When I was in that horrible heat, I thought about those ants. No matter how much water I drank, I felt like my body was an old dried up sponge. I did not see a drop of sweat the entire week and I could not wait for class to be over in the evenings so I could take off my shoes and put on flip-flops.

I love to wear sneakers and mules, but my feet felt like someone held a magnifying glass to my toes. With cool showers and a good night's rest, I was refreshed each new day for class.

My cohort group had two wonderful professors and no methodologist. Those women looked like they were from a scene in a scary movie. They were pulled and tugged in different directions. Their heads whipped around because learners needed what seemed at the time to be urgent attention.

One day the topic of our grade point average (GPA) came up in class. This was the second time someone mentioned GPA. "Don't worry about your GPA," each professor said. "It doesn't matter." The entire class erupted at the same time, "It matters to me!" One of the professors pointed and wished a B on us for our next course.

Your GPA is extremely important, only because it will keep you from getting kicked out of your program. In terms of earning your doctorate or Ph.D., it does not matter. You will not be Dr. 4.0, you will be Dr. (Insert your name here). I was so hung up on my GPA, I did not want to accept a B in any course, no matter what.

When I took my statistics class, I had to learn the data analysis program the woman simulated earlier with her fingers. I was grateful for the B+ I earned. From that class forward, I did not worry about a B. By the time I graduated, I had three B's on my transcript, and guess what? I still do not care. Do not get hung up on your GPA. If you feel your grade is unfair, go through the proper channels to appeal it, otherwise, drive on!

We worked hard. Every learner had their outline aligned and prepared to present. By the last day of class, we talked about everything except class. Our professors answered questions and gave us advice on what to do next in our learning journey. I implemented everything they told us, but nothing worked as I had hoped.

The days were long but very much worth it. The residency concluded, my study aligned, and I readied to go home and work hard to get through the remainder of my coursework. I was on my way to becoming a doctor driving my bus... or, so I thought! Slam on the brakes.

Choosing A Topic

What I have to say to you in choosing a topic for your dissertation is important. I went into my first residency with my topic already chosen. It was a topic I was passionate about and wanted to research, but my passion proved not to be enough by any standards. Unlikely, but several students were afraid someone would steal their topic; therefore, reluctant to provide detail or to share. It did not concern me in any way about my study because like always, I was the outlier. Even if someone stole your topic, they would not conclude the same results.

Ten people could repeat your study, conduct their research in the same parameters, and the findings would not come out the same. It is not as simple as taking a topic and conducting research, it is far too analytical. By the time the residency ended, I had my topic "aligned." I placed the word "aligned" in quotations because I had chosen a topic, but no one asked me if I had a gap or need statement. No one explained what a gap or need statement for the study was or where to find one.

I showed up with my topic sentence, and my study was aligned from there. What I thought was the gap was not. I chose a study that was done on sighted individuals because I wanted to do the same study on the blind. I thought that was the gap or need statement that would drive my dissertation. I had a discussion with another learner and explained why I chose my study. She said, "Oh, that's your gap." No, it was not my gap. Why I was listening to another learner is something I could never explain.

Nowhere in my chosen study did it say there was a recommendation for more research to be done on blind individuals. It did not ask for a replicated study either. I was driving my bus and had no idea where I was going. Since I could not find the gap or need for more research, there was no way I could have done my research. This lack of knowledge bit me later in my second residency.

The next few paragraphs are so important that when you are finished reading them, I want you to put down this book and find an empirical article or dissertation to read. I want you to see what I am telling you for yourself. If you do not know what an empirical article is, here is your chance to test your research skills. If I can save one learner by having them understand what I am saying, then my job is done, and you do not have to read any further.

What is the gap or need statement you ask? It is a recommendation for future research. You will find recommendations in Chapter 5 of every dissertation. You will find these recommendations in the discussion or conclusion sections of an empirical article. Not all articles are the same so thoroughly read them. Your university may not call it a gap or need statement but following my advice will help you find this critical information.

I encourage novice researchers to use a search engine of their choice to find articles. Type the topic you want to research in the search bar. Read any and all peer-reviewed articles or dissertations you find useful. You may also put PDF or DOI at the end of the search term. Here is an example of what your search might look like. *Why are trees green? DOI* or *Why are trees green? PDF.* If nothing shows up, you may have to tailor your search.

Make sure your document is three to five years old. My article could not be older than five years. Some professors preferred three years. It will take you several years to produce your dissertation. Try to find the latest research document as possible. Once you locate it, and it is the one you are likely to use, go to chapter five of the dissertation or if you use an article, go to the conclusion or discussion sections. Read the entire chapter or sections.

Some researchers distribute recommendations for future research throughout the chapter. Some may place it in specific areas such as the discussion, limitations, conclusion, or recommendations for future research sections. Find everything the researcher says when it comes to more research. Copy and paste the information to a new document or write each recommendation down in the order you find them.

It must say, "A need for more research. Suggested research. Recommendation for more research." Ideally, statements which call for more research or phrases which say more research should be conducted offer the best options. Read each recommendation carefully. You can only choose one so decide which one best suit what you want to research. If you do not find your interest in one article or dissertation, keep searching until you do.

When you chose your gap or need, you can construct your topic sentence, your problem statement, your purpose statement, your research questions, and the hypothesis if your study is quantitative. You are now beginning to use your skills to become a fine-tuned researcher.

When you are familiar with how to find your articles, use scholarly websites. You should also use your institution's library and ask librarians. If you attend a university where you are not allowed to use resources outside of your institution's library, this information still applies.

The purpose of finding and using a gap or need statement is to "fill in the gap or need" left by the researcher you chose. You will fill this gap or need by conducting your own research. Your research will answer their questions. It will also supply extra information that will help their research topic remain current.

When your dissertation is completed, you will have gaps or needs of your own. Someone might read your research and decide to fill your need or gap. They will do this by following the recommendations you listed in your study. You can fill your own gap or need by doing another study if you wish. You will have new answers to your questions, and it will keep the research current.

Programs have a time frame. Keep it simple and try to stay away from mixed methods research. Choose a study you can do within the period of your doctoral program. I saw learners kicked out of their program or handed an Education Specialist (Ed.S.) degree because they did not finish their program in a specified period. When you get your three letters, Ph.D. or Ed.D., you can go out and conquer the world with studies that take years.

I am not saying to produce subpar work. Your dissertation will reflect you, your committee, your university, and your participants. Take pride in your work and show respect to the process. Once you find your gap or need statement, you will use it to align your research. This will produce a strong dissertation. I used the word align several times already, but what is it?

Aligning is making sure each point of your dissertation has a strong relationship with each other. Alignment not only refers to your dissertation but also to your program. I have seen learners make it all the way to their first review with a perfectly aligned document. The document was kicked back because it was not aligned with their program emphasis. They either had to start their study over or find an article to save it.

Do not choose an architecture program and do a study on "How to Set A Dinner Table." Save that for a hospitality program. A proper dissertation would be "How to Design a House." Your dissertation committee should ensure your document is aligned. You are responsible for making sure your document gets into alignment and stays in alignment. Each university may have its own criteria for aligning. Be certain to check this important skill so you can produce a strong dissertation.

One professor during my first residency told me I was driving my bus. You heard me refer to this phrase already. I will refer to it during the rest of this book. Often, I had no idea where my bus was going, or whether the accelerator, steering wheel, or brakes worked.

Learners get frustrated, fearful, or angry when they cannot do a study, they wanted to conduct research on. I tweaked my topic several times during the years I was trying to complete my study. After the third year, I had to start from scratch. Emotions abound when a learner does not know what they are doing. When there is a member of their committee that is indifferent or does not give adequate feedback, it makes it more difficult.

If you have a chairperson who suggests you reword, change, or tweak your topic sentence, please be willing to do it. The most important thing is your population. I knew I wanted to do a study on the blind or visually impaired population. When I chose my first topic, my third committee member told me, one word in my topic sentence was too general. I took the word out but kept my population.

You have the right to fight for your topic. If you can justify it, discuss it with your chairperson. If you cannot justify it, stop wasting precious time. Holding on to your population is the most crucial element, do not stress over a trivial issue.

I learned how to write my literature review during coursework. The course was invaluable. Though the literature review was hard to write, it was the section I learned the most about my conceptual frameworks and my topic. My enrollment advisor told me I would start to write my dissertation during my coursework. I did, but by the time I got to my first dissertation course, I did not have any part of my dissertation started. Every professor after my literature review course annihilated it with constant requests to re-edit. I had to start writing the literature review over. That part of marketing was inaccurate. It took months to complete another literature review.

As you progress in your program, you will witness a change in your ability to write academically. What you start with will be unrecognizable with the constant editing you will have to do. One of my biggest issues was the American Psychological Association (APA) formatting. Every professor wanted the format completed differently. I became insecure about this skill. If you remember, I mentioned earlier that one of my professors said I had a different way of writing which was unique.

This professor informed me they have academic discretion. Professors can use their discretion at any time when they were grading. Though APA has specific rules, what one professor requested was rejected by another. It became my weakness during writing. If this is your kryptonite, use tools available to help you with your writing. At this level of learning, you must write scholarly.

Research Tips

Everyone has a way of studying that helps them retain information. As a doctoral or Ph.D. learner, you will not study, but you will be in a constant mode of learning, researching, and writing. I am going to provide you some valuable tips that will not be presented in any specific order. I used these tips during my journey, and I hope they help you during yours.

Earlier, I talked about the need to look through empirical articles. I did not understand the value of comparing and contrasting until I got into the literature review course. Synthesizing requires finding a large number of documents. You must take these documents and combine them, so they can support your study.

This is a difficult skill to master that you must learn. I can look at a learner's document and tell if they have good synthesizing skills by the amount of in-text citations and references they have. If I see the same citation used constantly or if I see a short reference list, I annotate a number I believe the learner should have and ask them to find more resources.

In some of my courses, I felt like I wrote every day for weeks when papers were only due every two weeks. As I moved to the dissertation part of my program, synthesizing became easier and I recognized the value of the first two courses I took when I started the program.

As you construct your dissertation chapters, you will repeat information. When I chose my final gap statement, I wrote it several times. Each time I wrote my gap statement, I reworded it. I copied and pasted the gap sentence to a new document so that I would not write it the same way throughout my dissertation. I developed pages full of my reworded gap statement.

My problem statement, purpose statement, and research questions remained the same throughout my document. During your writing, you will repeat information in different chapters. This is to inform readers what your study addressed if they decided to pick up one chapter to read instead of the entire dissertation. No one reads a dissertation for the fun of it. I could barely stand to read my own. I have not read it since I received my bounded copy. Please get used to repeating information throughout the five chapters.

You may read so much literature that finding resources might become difficult due to saturation. Lack of available research is another reason you may have a difficult time finding resources. My topic was different, so finding resources was difficult. Look in the reference section of the articles you chose and use those. If references are too old, cross-referencing, and secondary resources may yield current resources.

When you choose your theoretical foundation or conceptual framework, reach out to the researcher. I chose four conceptual frameworks, and one theory over the span of time I conducted my research. Each researcher responsible for the theory or conceptual framework responded when I reached out to them. I keep in contact with one to this day. Some of those researchers may want to help you and others might be too busy, but reach out if you can.

There are encyclopedia websites you can use. You will not be able to use the website as a reference or citation but I found one of these forbidden websites to be invaluable. At the bottom of each page is usually a treasure trove of references; use them. When I researched my conceptual frameworks and theories, this website supplied a lot of excellent information that I used. If I could not use the references, the information led me to other resources for me to use.

Finding innovative ways to create your study is part of a researcher's method. I know if a professor read this book, he or she would become horrified by reading this tidbit. It worked for me, and it will work for you. Pay attention to what you read. Someone gave me the perfect article to use in my dissertation. This conceptual framework could not have been more perfect. I completed my dissertation but had to remove every in-text citation and reference. We did not realize it was a master's thesis. Since a master's thesis cannot support a dissertation, I could not use it. He was one of the researchers I tried to reach out to when I chose his conceptual framework, but I did not get a reply until I had completed my dissertation. This researcher is in Uganda and was beyond thrilled someone had chosen his work.

I prefer to read printed information. When I started to research literature, I printed every article I could. I threw each article in a box next to my bed but printing soon became prohibitive. If printing is a prohibitive cost, create a folder in your email and send every digital article you find to it. I created several folders during my journey to save approved documents, iterations to my committee, eBooks, and anything I felt the need to make them for.

My chairperson told me each phase of my dissertation was like building a wall. Each stage was a new layer of bricks I added to my wall. Once I got my document approved, I was not to remove anything. I was only supposed to add to it. This was impossible since every time I sent it to an editor, the document changed.

When I got to the last stretch of my journey, my completed dissertation was different from my first phase. My document was kicked back because of the unapproved changes. I had to find the original document, so I could copy and paste the approved information to the final dissertation. Since I had the documents saved in its own folder, it was easy for me to copy and paste the original and approved information back into the document.

After you work on your document, save it by the name of the course, date, and time. Never save your document solely by course and date. I cannot tell you how many times I sent my third chairperson the wrong document because I did not provide a time stamp.

I sat for hours and worked on my document and saved it with the same tag I used for the earlier document. When it was time to send my iteration, instead of sending the latest document, I accidentally sent the older version. I felt badly when I forwarded the wrong document. It appeared to my chairperson as if I had not made corrections she instructed me to fix.

Be advised, do not depend on your computer to provide a time stamp. Hit "save as," tag it, send it to yourself and save it to a designated folder. The filename should look something like this: Theory07242018413p.m.

Pay attention to what you typed, and where you saved your document. I saved a research paper and I could not find it because I saved it to the wrong place. I also mistyped a word by one letter. My computer had no idea what I asked it to find. I was fortunate to have a compassionate professor who allowed me to hand in the document the next day.

Save your folders to the cloud service of your choice. You can keep a copy of your articles, or dissertations on your desktop but if your computer crashes, you are going to be a very unhappy person. Save your documents to your email or cloud for another benefit. You can work on your research papers and dissertation documents during your lunch breaks.

Learners who reached out to me while they were at work received unwelcome news from their committee members and needed my help. To ease their panic, I asked them to send their document to me so I could review it and offer advice. Some said they had to wait until they got home because the document was on their home computers. Between that time, they were frantic with worry. If you save your document in your email folders or cloud, you can send it any time someone requests it.

As I got closer to finishing my dissertation, I used two computers for my research. I used one computer to conduct my research and write. I used the other computer to check my emails. I also used two different operating systems. When I sent iterations to my chairperson, an issue with incompatibility surfaced. Information or images I was able to send from one computer would not make it to my chairperson's computer. Use the suggested operating system of your university. I used one operating system when I traveled. When I completed my iterations, I sent my document to my email, checked it on the other operating system, and then sent it to my chairperson.

One of the most valuable assets is your university librarians. Use the librarians when you experience difficulty finding material to support your research topic. Do not make it a habit of automatically asking for help. The more you try to find resources on your own, the better researcher you will become.

This next tip is not a popular one. Go to your public library to find material which has several benefits. It will get you into some fresh air and sunshine, provide you some much-needed exercise and it will keep you from spending excessive amounts of hours locked up in a room away from human contact.

At the beginning of my program, I was the super doctoral learner. I bought every interesting book I could find on how to write a good dissertation, how to create the literature review and I did not read one book on the topic. I had so many books that when I was tried to sell them, I discovered I had two copies of some of the same books.

Buying books proved to be a waste of my hard-earned money. Your dissertation is a living, active, ever-changing document and no book can tell you how to write it. The only people who can guide you on writing your dissertation are your committee members, or whoever the university put in charge of your process.

The only books I would encourage a leaner to buy are books that discuss the proper use of APA at the current level, notebooks, books on your methodology, and your research design. This will help you to understand their history, their nature, and how to conduct your data collection.

There are specific rules about the use of et al. in APA. Learners do not always apply the use of et al. properly. With constant rewrites and a document well over two hundred pages, I often forgot to address this issue in my dissertation.

One day I decided to go through my entire document. I got a pen and a notebook. I went through each page and wrote down every citation that had three or more researchers. I also wrote the page number. Each time I saw the full citation after the first time, I knew I had to change the citation to the proper et al. format.

When I work with learners and see this issue, I asked them to use this tip, and it has never failed them. You can use the search feature in your word processing program, but reading the document will allow you to address other issues you may have missed. Please refer to your APA manual or a website to aid you with the proper use of et al.

The tip I am about to give you may not pertain to your university requirements. If it does, this tip will save you a lot of aggravation. Buy a cheap notebook. Do not use this notebook for anything except citations. You do not do this for every article you find, only the ones you will use in your study. Write down the researchers listed in the article. Write down what the article or dissertation is about. Write down the methodology, the design, and how many participants the researcher used. Write down each instrument (interview questions, questionnaires, surveys etc.).

Write down what the researcher used to collect their data (recording devices, telephone, video conferencing, dictation programs etc.). Write what the researcher used to analyze the data. Write what the article is about. Write how the researcher showed reliability and or validity. If your articles are missing any of these elements you will say, the researcher did not discuss it in the study.

Keep this notebook aside in case you need this information later. This might seem like a lot of work in the beginning. However, if this is required for your proposal, it will be much easier than having to go through articles to find this information later. Trust me!

At some point in your journey, I recommend hiring a good editor. Before you hire an editor, check with your university to see if they offer free editing services. Editors are easy to find, but many will charge you an arm and a leg with no guarantee they will do a decent job. Even if you have the best editor, when you have several people looking at your document, their opinions will differ.

Due to this fact, hiring an editor will not guarantee approval of your document and can become expensive if you must keep hiring one. It is better to hire a good editor than to pay for extra courses because your APA formatting, headings, figures, and tables are incorrect. If you decide to hire an editor, try to hire one by word of mouth. Ask a lot of questions about their services, and what they offer.

I hired several editors during my process. Some were great, some were not so good, and one I could no longer use. She was a professor at the university, and it was considered a conflict of interest. My first editor is the person who worked on this book. She could not help me in the beginning because she had no knowledge of my first topic. Well, no big deal there; neither did I. With the little amount of writing I had managed to do, her feedback was not supportive, but I kept driving my bus.

Several months later when I found my footing, I went back to her. My chairperson refused to check my work until I hired an editor. I could hear the frustration in her feedback. I had to hire an editor whether I wanted to or not. Whether I could afford one or not.

My university had a required number of pages for the literature review. There was no getting around it. It took months of research and writing for me to meet the minimum requirement. I sent my document to the editor. After checking it over, she sent me an invoice which I paid promptly. My editor was a fast worker, and she sent the document back within a few days. When I got my document back, she cut half of the pages. I had no time to stress over it. I had two days to make up the required pages.

Once I completed the required literature review pages, I realized why my chairperson kicked my work back. I also saw why the editor cut out so many pages. Though I had a lot of information, it was a lot of fluff that was not concise. Though APA is important, APA will not matter if your document is poor in content. Hire yourself a good editor.

I used a website to create a reference list. The website helped format my references and it will help you format yours. If it takes you fifty years to graduate, do not erase any references until your dissertation has been published. Create a bibliography as you add information and save it to a folder in case the website goes down.

Research Tips

Before my committee forwarded my dissertation to the dean, I had an issue with missing citations and references. As the years pass in your learning journey, you will do so much editing that you may lose track of citations and references. I had references with no in-text citations or in-text citations with no references.

I hired an editor who attended my university. I believed she knew exactly what to do to address the issues. The editor did an excellent job on my tables, figures, and headings. The APA formatting was poor, and I got my dissertation kicked back several times. After firing her, I decided to struggle through on my own. Since I had my bibliography, I found references and re-created citations I had long forgotten.

Upload your dissertation or research papers to a program that allows you to check your references. It will also check your in-text citations for proper formatting. This website has color prompts that will alert you to issues. Do this while going through your phases. Do not wait until you get to the end of your program or it will become overwhelming.

After your hard work, your dissertation committee will forward it for approval, signature, and prepared for publication. The last thing in the world you will want to do is re-read your dissertation. Read your dissertation! Redact all signatures, names, numbers, and locations and send it to someone you trust to read it.

You must read it as well. Even though it is your dissertation, you are going to miss a lot of issues. Fresh eyes will catch many mistakes you missed. Years ago, a famous talk show host who I love to hear orate, gave some advice that I will never forget. She said, "Whenever you write something, always let someone read it." When I received my dissertation from the dean, I read the entire two hundred and eighty-plus page document.

I wanted no part of reading it, but I had too. I sent it to two people who were brave enough to read it with me. I was appalled at the issues I found in my dissertation. Hiring an editor, trying to fix it myself, going through formatting and having the dean "read" and sign it, did not address every issue.

Read your own work! Your dissertation will be placed in the Library of Congress as a bounded book. If a potential employer wants to order a copy of your research, they will be able to do so. If you allow free access to your dissertation, everyone in the world will be able to see it. If you have a nosy neighbor, they will be able to read it. Once it is printed, it is out there forever. It might have small issues like typos, but things could be much worse.

DURING MY DOCTORAL STUDIES

Mind, Body, Spirit

During my program, there were times I knew I was in a living nightmare. There were days I wanted to take my faithful computer and send it sailing across the room. I hated researching when I was unable to find resources and I had to find a way to cope with my frustration. Below are some things I did to make my journey tolerable.

While going through your journey, you should always take some time to focus on your mind, body, and spirit. It is important to keep a balance between the stressors of your journey and your life. If one of these elements is out of order, it will affect the others.

Your mind, body, and spirit are deeply connected. They are our best friends and I listen to them when they speak to me. I hope these tips help you as much as they helped me.

MIND

Some people enjoy quiet surroundings while others an atmosphere with a lot of noise. Some people enjoy working inside while others prefer to work in nature. I cannot write in dead silence and found when I did, my mind ran amok. If the weather allowed, I went outside early in the morning and listened to my tiny-running-electric pond. I listened to chirping birds. Sometimes, I went to the coffee shop at 5 a.m. to buy a hot caramel macchiato and an orange-cranberry scone. Tea is my beverage of choice, but foofoo coffee gave me energy. It made me blissful and allowed me to write.

You will need to find time to have a normal life, especially if you work full-time. Working full-time and doing my doctoral program was difficult at best and a struggle. I would not head to bed until after midnight, and then have to wake up at 5:30 a.m. to get ready for work.

The best days to write were on the weekends, but what about my personal life? When did I spend time with my family? When did I have fun? When did I socialize? At some point, you must put down the books and say enough.

My assignments were due once a week. I did not pick up my new assignment until the day after my previous assignment was due. On the weekends I gathered the family and drove out of town for dinner at a different ethnic restaurant on each trip. I found myself becoming frustrated with my children while I tried to work on my studies. They invariably made teenager kinds of noises. I used to yell, "Don't knock on my door unless the house is on fire!" without considering what I spoke into the atmosphere.

I did not want my family to go through this experience with me and look back on it with disdain. The outings provided the perfect distraction for us. Do your work away from family distractions if you have an extra room. Allow your family their space and give yourself an allotted time each day to work. For me, four hours was the most I would write, but I broke my rule often.

I want you to grasp this next tip. It is important for you to heed this advice. I call them my "What if" tips. If you find yourself unable to think clearly if you cannot explain something coherently, if you are reading the same sentence over and over because you cannot understand it, then it is most likely you have writer's block. To combat writer's block, walk away from the computer and the books. This is your mind warning you to let it get the rest it needs. The more you research or write when your mind is tired, the more stress you will experience. Stressors erupt quickly and without warning.

When your mind is rested, it will let you know because fresh ideas start to flow, and you will be able to work without issue.

If you are a procrastinator, you are going to be in big trouble. Procrastination will not help productivity. It will get a learner into some serious issues. In my master's program, I was a student who procrastinated with perfection. I did it because the stress of waiting until the last minute forced my mind to think. It did not work in my program. I had to learn how to organize and prioritize.

If you attend residency collect the names of your classmates. Create a study group in your area. Go on social media and create a group. Keep the group secret or closed. This will allow learners to vent without spying eyes having access to who is saying what. Your university will always have someone on social media looking to see if people are speaking against them. A group will help with the loneliness you are guaranteed to feel. It will also supply you with much-needed support.

Before I started my doctoral journey, I was an avid reader. There was not a moment anyone would see me without a book and a mug full of green or ginger tea. I loved the smell, feel, and the sound of pages turning. When I walked into a bookstore, it made me happy. I felt like I floated on a cloud in slow motion every time I stepped inside one. It was even better if the bookstore had a coffee shop with red velvet cheesecake.

I stopped reading for pleasure for five years. I read so many articles during my studies, it took my desire to read away. I switched to audiobooks which allowed me to listen to the words, music, and the sound of the person who narrated put my mind in a place of bliss which also rested my weary eyes. If reading is something you can escape to during your studies, then read if you cannot invest in some audiobooks.

Sleep, oh wonderful, glorious, sleep. I wondered if I should put the topic of sleep under mind or body. I chose to include it under mind because I know exactly when I need sleep. I always took showers before bed to clean off the gunk of the workday. I would not dare sit on my furniture or bed without removing my clothing. Nightly showers, moisturizing lotion or a light layer of oil allowed my body to relax and to fall asleep.

I also took showers in the morning during the hotter months to wake up. One winter morning I prepared for work. I washed my face and brushed my teeth, I dressed, beat my face to perfection, fixed my hair, and spritzed on some perfume.

As I gave myself the once-over in the bathroom mirror, I noticed some glitter powder on my décolletage. I wore those powders to match my clothing and knew I had not dusted any on myself that morning. My eyes widened as saucers when I realized I did not take a shower the night before, nor that morning. I came home from work, started working on my dissertation, and forgot to take a shower. I had fifteen minutes to get out the door.

My clothing flew one way, and I flew in another direction. I got in and out of the shower as fast as I could. I detested rushing because it is one of the most negative emotions. I rushed that morning which left me in a state of panic and worry at every stop light because I did not want to be late for work.

Every day I returned home for a lunch break. I watched my soap, had some lunch, and allowed my dogs to run around in the yard. One day I went back to work and could not remember if I had left the stove on or if I turned it off.

I called my son and asked him to return to the house to check. He did, and I had. He also told me I left my dogs in the backyard. I never left my dogs out of their kennel when I left my house. Did I set the alarm? Did I lock the doors? Did I put the food in the refrigerator? Anytime I started to forget things, it signifies that my mind is worn out due to lack of sleep.

I went grocery shopping every weekend on Saturday or Sunday mornings. I wanted to be at the store between 5 a.m. and 6 a.m. I enjoyed shopping at that time. There were always great sales, and I did not have to battle with anyone except boxes which cluttered the aisle while stockers worked. I could get all my shopping done in an hour and leave.

One morning I was exhausted, but I just had to go to the store anyway. I stood in the fruit and vegetable section and walked a few steps away from my cart to get an item. I put the item in "my" cart and started pushing it. A woman came after me, "Ma'am! Ma'am! that's my cart."

I looked at her, glanced at the cart, and then fixated my eyes on hers as I apologized. Extremely embarrassed, I wanted the floor to open and swallow me right there on the spot. To my horror, I grabbed the wrong cart and left my wallet and items in the other one.

When I lacked sleep, it affected the way my mind functioned. It affected my awareness when I drove. It affected the way my body functioned, and it affected my spirit. Sleep is not a matter of closing your eyes and to dream. Sleep allows our minds to decompress, and our bodies to heal. When we get a cut or scrape on our body, it heals faster in the time of sleep than when we go about through our day.

I invested in a sleep monitor bracelet. Over the time I was in school, I eventually started going to bed at 9 p.m. I needed to get at least eight hours of sleep to function. When I checked my monitor every morning, I saw that I slept for eight hours but I had only rested for three or four hours. That explained why I was always tired and in a constant mental fog.

Leave a notebook and pencil next to your bed. When my mind was rested, I became inspired. What I wanted to write flowed during my sleep. I would have to wake up and start writing without hindrance until sleep took me away into soundness again. You must get the deep, restful, uninterrupted sleep you need. Never allow this journey or the stress of it, to deprive you of it.

BODY

When I started my journey, I worked a full-time job. I sat all day, stared into a computer screen and munched on "healthy" snacks; I beefed up. After six years, I lost my job due to cutbacks. Earlier in the year, I had a dangerous health crisis which I addressed later in this book. I was not willing to quit my job because I had bills to pay.

Mind, Body, Spirit

It was not until that time that I started feeling uncomfortable with the size of my body. I made the decision to go into the new year with weight loss goals. In January 2015, I hired a personal trainer who smacked talked me three days per week for five months to get me in tune with my weight loss goals.

Paying attention to what I put inside my body and working out with my trainer helped me lose twenty pounds. I started to take time to care for my body. It gave me more confidence, it allowed me to concentrate, and it affected my spirit and my mind in positive ways.

If one thousand people who are reading this right now, I predict a collective groan with my next sentence. You must find time to exercise; and here come the groans. I hear you! You can walk, jog, run, bounce on a rebounder, lift weights, stand on a vibrating machine, jump rope, swing a kettlebell, and join a gym or a boot camp. Your choice and the type of exercise are endless.

Find whatever you like to do and get your body moving and the sweat flowing. Drink fresh water and take vitamins daily and get your yearly checkups. Do whatever you can to focus on creating a better you. I aspired to become a doctor, and I wanted to look like one too. Working out allowed my mind to think better, and it gave me a lot of energy.

Every spring I had my nails manicured and maintained until the fall and I received pedicures on special occasions. Having someone scrub the bottom of my feet made me feel like I am about to go into orbit with the overwhelming tickling that terrorizes my entire body. I skip them unless I am going to be wearing shoes that bare my toes.

After 2015, I could not afford to get my nails done anymore. Even if I had money for this luxury, I would not take the time to spend one to two hours away from my dissertation.

No matter how bad things get, there are a few things in a woman I feel should never change. She should always look neat, have a beautiful smile, and she should always have a beautiful attitude. Regardless of how hard things got for me, I always maintained my neat appearance, I always carried a smile even if I had to force one and I had a beautiful attitude even when I was feeling like my heart would implode with grief or despair. Then, at one point I was so consumed with my journey that I neglected those simple things that brought me joy.

You must take care of your best friend (body) and your temple from the inside and the outside. Getting my hands and feet manicured was not important, but it would have given me a break. I became consumed with my journey because no matter how hard I tried; I did not progress.

It would have been easy to go to the store to buy nail polish to brighten up my hands and feet, and subsequently would have gotten me out of my house allowing me to get fresh air and sunshine. Most importantly it would have gotten me away from my dissertation.

I went back to get my nails done for graduation after three long years. When my nail tech was done, he said, "Now you don't look like a tomboy."

I said, "Yeh!" and we both started laughing.

SPIRIT

I am a very spiritual woman, a Christian who believes in the power of prayer. I will not focus on any specific religion. What I want you to focus on is using your spirituality to help you progress. If you have none, find some. You are going to need it.

I believe in visualization and to stay positive as much as possible. There was a period in my journey when my faith was shattered. I could neither pray nor did I want to as I felt God had abandoned me and I saw no evidence of his word in my life. Things kept getting worse with 2015 through 2017 being some of the most difficult years of my life. I am extremely happy that I will never have to see them again.

In 2014 my daughter attended a photography class. Her assignment was to take pictures of her family members. I do not like taking pictures, but I wanted to help her, so I allowed her to. She took my picture and made a postcard. She gave it to me, and it said, "Happy Holidays Dr. Davis." In 2014 I was nowhere near being awarded the title of Dr. Davis.

I told my daughter I would keep the postcard on my refrigerator door as my daily reminder of my goals and it became my visualization to reach them. It also reminded me of the faith this beautiful, positive, teenager had in her mother which I cherished.

Another day I went through my social media page and saw a graphic with three graduation robes. In the comment section, my daughter said, "Soon my mom will have all three." Again, I was nowhere near the title of Dr. Davis. Many days over the following years, I stood in front of my refrigerator with tears streaming down my face. I often desired to pull the postcard off the door, rip it into long thin strips and discard them because of my struggles in my doctoral journey. The fact that my daughter had faith in me kept my spirit hopeful and that postcard was my visualization reminder. The love she showed by making the postcard was stronger than my desire to destroy it. I still have it on the refrigerator door, and there it will stay.

In the back of this book, I included visualization graphics for you. I want you to remove them and tape a picture of your face on it. Write your name on the diploma and place these graphics in an area where you can see them every day; a bathroom mirror or refrigerator door would be ideal. There will be days when you will feel like you will never meet your goal. When you look at these graphics, it will remind you that you can push through anything in your journey. Remember, you are in control of your bus and its destination.

When I was at the lowest point of my journey, I envisioned myself walking across the graduation stage dressed in my regalia. No one was with me, no fanfare, no pictures, no handshaking and there was no cheering. I was alone in a huge auditorium, but I walked across that stage anyway. In my mind, it gave me the courage to continue when I felt I was fighting a losing battle.

I secluded myself from people who upset me and from things, and situations filled with negativity. I wanted to remain in a place of peace and positivity, and I wanted no extra stress. Every day I found one thing to be grateful for even if it was the fact that I had opened my eyes, my feet were able to walk, and I could go to work.

When anyone walked into my humble and cozy home, I wanted peace and serenity to greet them. When I researched and wrote, I always lit candles around me. Candles, whether scented or unscented change the atmosphere of any room with aromatherapy –a proven fact to ease stress. I also love pink Himalayan salt lamps and have several in my home.

Being around running water puts me in a place of pure serenity. I bought a larger water fountain that I plugged in every day during spring and summer. During the evenings, I plugged in the light which changed the water to a beautiful royal blue color. Spiritual music such as soft meditation, gospel, soft instrumentals, or 70s music spoke to my soul, so I played it too.

I am not an advocate of lying, but here are some things I want you to say daily as affirmations. Say them more often when you feel like things are hopeless. *"Something good is just about to happen to me,"* and *"Today brings me one day closer to my miracle."*

There were days when no person could tell me things were going to get better and I felt like a liar saying these affirmations. If I did not want to say them, I thought them. I was in a deep hole for so long I was certain I would stay there, and I resigned myself to it. There was another phrase I kept reminding myself of when I was at my absolute lowest. This phrase was my mantra of choice. *"God did not send me here to fail."*

These affirmations have power! Your words have power! Say them until you believe them! Say them until your spirit starts to feel better! Create your own mantra if you must. It will get better. I promise you it will, but you must at all costs remain positive. Nothing stays the same forever. You will come out of your darkness, but you must focus on your light no matter how dim it is.

Think of those things that bring peace to your spirit and your workspace. If you love soft music or instrumentals, then play music. Pray over your hands before you start working on documents. Make your workspace organized and cheerful. Your workspace is going to be cluttered while you work. Always leave it neat and organize when you are finished working for the day. Never leave it cluttered as it can stress you out when you start working again the next day.

If you like the scent of incense, burn some. Buy a diffuser or put a pot of water on the stove, sprinkle it with cinnamon, and let it simmer.

Wonderful smells change your mood. Think of the fresh smell of hot coffee while it is brewing, or your favorite foods while it is cooking. It does wonderful things to you, doesn't it?

Remove yourself from negative things, negative people, and negative situations. Keep yourself in a positive frame of mind. Remind yourself that everything you are dealing with is a part of the process and you will complete your journey.

If you feel like your mind, body, or spirit, are not where they should be, take the time to get all three back into balance. Focus on your family and your best friends. It is an extremely important aspect during your doctoral journey that many do not speak about. It helped me, and it will help you.

No Short Cuts

We all love a good shortcut, don't we? During your doctoral studies, you can find companies that provide shortcuts. They charge prices that might have you scratching your head. These services are willing to write your dissertation with little to no coaching. Some will give you a lot of coaching and other companies will even sell you a diploma. I now understand why these companies exist. I understand why they do well despite the money they charge and the deception they provide.

You are free to do this, but may I ask? Would it be worth your reputation, or monetary loss if someone found out? Rest assured that someone will find out. When they do the consequences can be devastating.

Picture yourself in the highest paying position you dreamed to obtain. After achieving your goal, you become comfy and cozy. Your credentials come into question and you lose your job. Will you be ready for the humiliation, loss of your income, or new lifestyle?

Even if you get through your dissertation defense or you get the job because someone did not take the time to check your credentials, there will always be that one thing that will not seem right. How anyone can buy a dissertation and get away with it is still a mystery to me, but it happens. Imagine one day you are in a group of coworkers while taking a break they start talking about their research. You have a cold refreshing drink in your hand sipping it while having big fun in conversation. They start asking you about your research. Will you retreat to your work area? Will you bury your head in your drink to squelch the heat that will radiate from your face and neck? Will your cold refreshing drink turn warm like the weather as your hands radiate heat? Will your tongue become twisted as you try to answer? Will you know how to answer? Someone is going to find out; do not consider it. These companies charge you a lot of money. Once you pay your money, they will not care if you get caught.

I have heard of learners who try to find others willing to write their dissertation and I have heard of others who were caught by the university. Learners have offered to pay me to author their research papers and dissertation chapters. I explained the unethical nature that it would be and explained the consequences associated with it. Additionally, I made certain to inform them how much appreciation they would miss by having someone else do their work. There is no self-gratification when others do your research or dissertation.

A nice pep talk and informing them how much faith and confidence I had in their abilities was all the encouragement they needed to continue. Never exchange your reputation or your moral compass to achieve your degree. There is an incredible amount of confidence, honor, and pride you will feel when you stand up in a room and show everyone you are the expert on your research.

Dissertation Committee

After two years of coursework I finally made it to my dissertation courses. I loved my coursework experience and learned a lot of wonderful information, but it was time to get to the meat. Every learner who made it to this point was extremely excited. I was supposed to have the first section of my dissertation done. It was as far from the truth as the sun is from the moon. I was still happy and excited because I made it with one year left to finish.

The dissertation part of my journey was unpleasant, and I will always have a void for not enjoying it. Please, do your best to enjoy your journey no matter how difficult it becomes.

Every university has guidelines for the members of your dissertation committee. My committee consisted of three people. The university chose two members, and I chose one. By the time I completed my program I had seven different committee members. One was interchangeable by switching roles. I had so many counselors, I do not remember the number.

My first chairperson was wonderful, friendly and responsive to my questions. At one point, some of us were unsure which document we were supposed to be working toward completion. My chairperson did not know either. What? When I asked her for a clarification, she told me to work on the wrong document and I did not find out until much later in my journey.

She was new to the university. I do not think she knew the process well. Other universities did not use some documents my university did. After a few weeks, we did not hear from her for almost two months. When she came back, she apologized by telephone and explained that it was due to technical issues with the university.

A few weeks after the next course started, there was radio silence again. I got a nonchalant phone call from my counselor who informed me I was assigned a new chairperson. There was neither a word on why my former chairperson left nor did I recognize any sign she would be leaving. When I received my new chairperson, I welcomed him to the class and was ready to work hard, but he came in like a tempest.

I sent my iterations as required. One day the new chairperson asked if I had my previous document approved. I told him I had not, and I was working on the document the other chairperson instructed me to work toward completion. It *was* the wrong document. He told me to immediately stop working on it and to work on the correct one.

I worked until the end of the class on that document with no success. The next course started and there was a form I had to complete. Great, another form to complete. I was about to take a shower when I decided to check my email. I received A's for filling out this form before. This chairperson gave me a C. This was my first C ever in my master's or doctoral program.

My reaction to this is comical now, but it was not comical then. When I stepped into the shower, I folded up in tears. It was an overly dramatic and horrible experience. All I saw was my GPA sliding down the shower drain and me getting thrown out of the university. I cried and left it alone. When I went into my virtual classroom, I lost it!

I was the learner who always said to remain positive and to be patient and who encouraged my peers. "We got this. We can't complain about our former chair to others. We liked her, give her a chance to come back and explain what happened. We do not want her to get into trouble." Well, I had finally run out of patience as I had been patient for over two months.

So, You Want To Be A Doctoral Learner Huh? ARE YOU NUTS?!

I was told without warning that I had a new chairperson. I became upset by it as I had been working on the wrong document for weeks. I wasted thousands of dollars and I was ticked. My response was as if the floodgates had opened. I did not use one word of profanity, but the caps lock on my keyboard was not big enough to express my virtual volume.

I decided the days as the patient learner was over. I contacted the university and requested a refund for the previous class. I did not request the refund within five weeks after the old class ended and they knew this before they told me to fill out the appeal form. There was nothing the university would do to help me even though I had proof the chairperson was not in class for two months. The university was the one that caused the issue but that did not matter to them and I was not getting a dime back. Lesson learned -- pay attention to the tuition reimbursement and guidelines for your university. I might say this more than once before you get to the end of this book because I am still affected by it. My university had rules they rarely broke. The rules were not in place to protect me, but there to protect the university. The employees verbalized every rule when they needed. Do not ever forget that.

When my third course started, the class of five turned into a class of two. We wondered what happened to the rest of the class cohorts. After bringing it up several times, the chairperson put a stop to our discussion. I eventually found out one learner had taken a short break, but I never found out what happened to the other two.

I requested a conference with my chairperson. We had a candid conversation about our expectations. He felt it was unfair the way he was treated when he came to the class. I felt it was unfair for him to come in the classroom like an abominable bull. I did not say it to him, but that was how I thought and felt. I welcomed him to the class, but I guess my virtual yelling made him forget.

I listened to him as he bragged about his accomplishments. He always made his level of education a point of conversation. In retrospect, I earned that C. My first chairperson graded my form wrong. It did not have the detailed information I was supposed to have included.

Some professors took that first form very seriously, so I made certain to pay attention to the tiniest detail.

Any reason the university had for me complete that form eluded me. All of my goals recorded on it went swooshing by with the speed of a downhill skier with each course. How I felt about it did not matter. The form had to be completed.

During the meeting with my chairperson, I shared my concerns and frustrations. He assured me I would graduate with my Ph.D. I did not care to correct him. At that point, he could call it whatever he wanted, so long as it had the word 'graduate' in the sentence. We had a good discussion, and I understood what I needed to do in order to go forward. He promised my document would not go to the methodologist until he was sure it would get approved. I listened to his instructions, and I did everything he asked. I wanted my document to be approved.

I worked hard to turn in a good document. It took a few weeks of fixing, sending, and re-submitting it to bring to his standards. I received the results from my chairperson. Success! My document was finally on the way to the methodologist and I was tickled cinnamon brown! I excitedly bounced around my house squealing with happiness. Finally, I was moving forward in my journey.

Remember, my chairperson told me he would not send my document forward until he was sure it would get approved. I could finally get some rest and be happy again. Thinking about it gave me a new pep in my step. I was not worried about the time I had to wait because I knew I had this in the bag.

One day while I was at work, I opened my email. The days of anticipation were over. I received results from the methodologist. Seeing her email made me nervous, but hopeful and I smiled. When I read the feedback, I felt like a balloon that had been blown up to maximum capacity and then released before anyone could tie it.

My methodologist cut my document into confetti. I could see my chairperson in my head laughing. He was successful in pulling off the biggest pranks ever. I was a sucker and did even know it. I did not cry, I did not fuss, and I did not get angry. I felt if I cried, it would give him satisfaction and that was the last thing I wanted to do.

I let it go and kept on driving my bus. I tried to convince myself that this person did not know what he was doing. I refused to believe he purposely tried to sabotage me. I could not accept that anyone could be so cruel.

He made a promise that turned out to be a blatant lie. I went through every page of my document to review feedback the methodologist provided. The feedback was outside of her role but it was much needed. That feedback should have come from my new chairperson. After reading the methodologist's feedback, it was so clear to me that I was able to understand what I was doing wrong. I deeply appreciated it.

Make sure to put forward your best effort to succeed and always remain professional when you bring complaints to your counselor, committee members or anyone at your university and calmly explain your concerns. In hindsight, I should not have lost my temper with my chairperson. Would things have been successful had I remained the submissive learner? No, but I do not like finding solutions in getting angry.

The sad part is, I did not feel sorry for any of it. If I had not gotten angry, no one would have listened. The submissive doctoral learner took a leave of absence. I learned to open my mouth and speak up for myself. I was too patient, and it worked against me. If I had spoken up right away, I would have gotten reimbursed for the class my chairperson missed for close to two months.

Committee members will require you to fix many details in your document before they approve your work. You will have so many changes you may feel like your study is no longer yours and after you change one thing, they will ask you to change it again, or change something else or go back to the original. Over and over they will ask you to make changes to the same document. Changes should never take months.

Committee members have a certain amount of days to return your iterations. You have due dates for your assignments. Two months to wait for communication or feedback is beyond unacceptable. Never allow your committee members to be late without speaking up. Send an email to ask if they are okay and remind them of their due date.

If you still do not hear from your committee member contact your counselor and have them reach out for you. Keep a record of each time you reach out and try to be compassionate. Your committee members are human, and things happen. There were times during my coursework when professors showed me compassion. I had no problem returning it.

I depended too much on my chairperson to provide guidance on what I should have done. I should have found a way to see if I worked on the right document or not. After all, it is my responsibility to learn. Unfortunately, we do not know what we do not know. I completed every assignment and took care of every task each chairperson instructed. Had I not, I knew my work would not go forward.

My non-reaction to the incident about my feedback from the methodologist may have bothered my chairperson. He kept kicking back my document to me without specificity. I had a section of in-text citations he kept saying was wrong. Each time he sent it back I asked what was wrong with it, checked it, and changed it. I could not see the issue. I changed my citations so much I was sure citations that were correct were now wrong. Every time he sent my document back, I would "fix" it.

Instead of sending the document back right away, he waited until his return due date. He sent it back with the same phrase saying that my citations were wrong. This went on for weeks and I could not see the problem. There was not much feedback on the other sections of the paper, except to say I had not written enough.

There was a section in my document that I had to write in a bulleted list. I was positive that this was the correct format because when the methodologist gave her feedback, this was how she informed me to complete that area. My chairperson did not want it written that way, he wanted it written in paragraph form. Despite my knowing this was wrong, I did what he told me to do. There is no way the methodologist would have approved it, but I did it anyway. I found myself going to a place of abject hate and I did not like the way I felt.

You may get a committee member who forgot what it was like to go through the same struggle you are now having; therefore, you must find ways to cope. Some professors will make it their mission to stop you from getting ahead, or at least it seems this way. The doctoral journey is the one place where your fate is in someone else's hands. You do as they say, or you suffer through your process.

I had a cohort member who wanted to conduct a study she was extremely passionate toward. She had someone willing to work with her when the rest of us did not know how to recruit or who we would use for our research. She had a lot of difficulties getting her documents approved. She felt two professors tried to completely change her study. She refused to make the corrections they asked for in her document. One professor told her if she did not change it, she would make sure her study did not get approved. This professor had the power to do it too. I am grateful no one dared threatened me in this way.

You might get committee members who are willing to go above and beyond to see you succeed. They will make sure their name ends up on your final dissertation, but a good committee member will not sign their names to foolishness. You are still going to have to work hard. When it comes to your chairperson you never know who you will get.

If you have good professors always let them know how much you appreciate them. I had so much respect for my final committee members. When I did not want to change something, I would express my rationale, If I failed at it, then I did what they suggested because I trusted them. I knew my study would not go forward until I followed instructions, but I also knew they always had the best in mind for my work and research.

Let us take a step back for a few minutes. Before you choose a university, find out if you can choose your chairperson. If you are fortunate to have the luxury to choose your chairperson, ask questions about their dissertation, how long they have been a chairperson, about their responsiveness to questions and ask whether they give feedback that is scant, or detailed. All of these questions will have a bearing on your outcome.

Also, you should ask about their success rate for the learners under their supervision to reach the defense of their dissertations. If you interview anyone and you feel that your race, ethnicity, gender, creed, cultural difference, or topic choice is going to be an issue, pass on that individual. If their degree emphasis does not align with your program, pass on them.

Some might say the program of your chairperson does not matter and only the knowledge to write the dissertation does. I strongly disagree. I worked on my doctorate in the area of leadership. My second chair had a Ph.D. in finance, and he did not earn his Ph.D. in the United States. Why was this chairperson in charge of me?

If you cannot choose your chairperson, find their contact information. Ask those questions before you start class. If you find anything objectionable, do not begin the class. At my online university the minute you clicked into the classroom, you paid for it. You were stuck with the chairperson and it took hell to get rid of one if you could.

I contacted one of my revolving door counselors and informed them I wanted a new chairperson, but all I heard from her was how many learners he helped to succeed. That was fine and dandy, but he was not helping me or any of my other cohort members. I had no proof of her assertion.

You might have a chairperson who is new to the process. A new university chairperson is not always a disqualifying factor. However, you should have someone who knows the process. Two of my chairpersons were new to the process, and one was not. This chairperson was well versed on the requirements of the university which worked in my favor. If there is anything that does not seem right to you, pass on the chairperson.

You cannot conduct a study if it is not supported by the Institutional Review Board (IRB). If you want to do a study on animals, ask the university. If the university does not support it, find another university, or change your topic. I saw this happen to one person who was in IRB for three years. He wanted to do a study on animals and children. He eventually accepted a lower degree.

If you choose a Christian university, do not choose a topic like *A Qualitative Phenomenological Study: The Lived Experiences and Goodness of Diablo*. Find another university. This is not the time to wage a moral, religious, or ethical battle. If someone asks you to change your study and they cannot justify why they are telling you to do it; fight for your topic. Before you fight that battle, make certain you can justify your topic with empirical research.

When you speak to an enrollment counselor ask if you must put the chairperson as your co-researcher on your dissertation. I would never attend a university where that is required. My university did not have this rule, but I met another person whose did.

I witnessed learners quit their programs because they could not get along with a member of their committee. This situation occurred in other universities and not just the one I attended. I did not like my chairperson and the university forced me to work with him. I was not making progress. I was being charged over $2,000 for each course. There were more classes I had to pay for out of pocket before completing the program.

Do not accept this type of situation. I spent over a year in an expensive doctoral program with a chairperson who was what I considered of the devil. I beseeched my counselors to move me away from my chairperson, or him away from me. No matter how much I pleaded or how high my complaint went up the chain, the answer was always no. No matter what, I had to make it work with my chairperson. Guess what? It was not working, and I felt I could not do anything about it.

I sent a copy of my document to the head of dissertation services. I asked her to look at the junk my chairperson had me write. The blame came back on me because I did not post on the right board. The message board was something the chairperson never complained about. It was new to the program. I did not understand how to use it, and it had nothing to do with my complaint. I had finally had enough. I went above every head I could and contacted board members with my complaints.

I prepared myself to report the university to every agency I could. I also signed up to be a part of a class action lawsuit. I did not mention the lawsuit in the letter, but I wrote down every agency I was going to contact. Someone listened because early the next morning, the director of the department called. I had met him before when they were trying to recruit me. He is a kind and funny man, but I was not in a joking mood.

He asked me to open another investigation and let my counselor know he was involved. I explained my frustration with the program, the broken promise of the length of the program, my chairperson who promised not to send my document forward until he was sure the methodologist would approve it, being forced to work with someone who was not helping me progress, the money I paid for each class and not having my complaints addressed by anyone. Finally, I told him I did not see a single person graduate with an Ed.D. or Ph.D. The only thing I saw was learners leaving with a receipt of D.E.B.T.

He asked if the document I had been working on for months was more than twenty pages. I said, "Yes, I think it's forty pages."

He said, "That document is only supposed to be ten to twelve pages long."

After I got off the phone, I opened my document and checked to be certain. It was over sixty pages of pure, unadulterated, junk that could not be approved no matter what I did.

I wrote until I ran out of words. With thousands of words in the English language, I could not think of one single word left to add. I never threw away my worthless document. I had someone bind it for me in 2014 and I still have it collecting dust. It was so bad that if I wanted to become a millionaire, all I would have to do was change the title to -- *How Not to Write the Dissertation*" and publish it. Years later, my third chair and I got a chuckle out of it. I had come a long way from those days.

Doctoral or Ph.D. programs are expensive and time-consuming. For someone to purposely hinder your progress is wrong and unacceptable. My chairperson did not care whether I succeeded or not. If someone has that attitude toward you, do your best to get help to fix the issue.

You may feel you have no recourse. If there is no one willing to help you within, then seek help outside the university. Do not walk away with a large amount of debt with nothing to show for it. Give your advisor and the university the chance to help you work things out before you go outside for help.

Always be professional. If you cannot be professional, ask for a mediator. If your committee members grade your work with little or unclear feedback, request a meeting. Ask for clarification to help you understand. One hindrance for me was the fact I was a visual and tactile learner. My background was in aviation and I was used to looking at and touching things.

Sometimes I need to see things to understand what I am doing. Online schooling was not always easy because of it. This does not mean that I am dumb. It means that I have a different learning style. My chairperson wrote some of his feedback in a way that was difficult to understand. He was not patient when it came to his feedback and often failed to explain what he meant by it, unlike my third chairperson. Even though you are earning your doctorate or Ph.D., you are still a "student." Never forget that and never allow anyone to make you feel dumb because of it.

Early in my program, I found some professors with a Ph.D. more difficult to work with than professors with an Ed.D. I am not sure what it was about, but it was my silent observation. Maybe they felt online schooling did not have the same respect or value as a brick and mortar school. This would be hypocritical since they were teaching at one.

Maybe it was because a Ph.D. is mired in heavy research and they expect the same from us. Maybe some do not find an Ed.D. holds as much value as a Ph.D. Who knows or cares? At the end of the road, both degrees must produce a dissertation, and both degrees will give you the title of Dr. in front of your name.

Some professors will expect you to research until you find the answers. They will not help you when you ask a question. Some professors may give you a hint. Some might tell you to figure it out. Do not take it personally. They are trying to get you to learn how to research. When learners asked me for help, I gave hints and asked them to find the answer. I wanted them to learn how to become stronger researchers.

My Second Residency

Two years after I attended my first residency, I prepared to attend my second residency. Like the first residency I made hotel, and my residency reservations. The only two exceptions; I did not take my children, and I went to a state in the southeast. I asked my reservation agent if I could arrive early. The agent told me I could. That was a colossal mistake.

I could not wait to get to the hotel so I could go to sleep. I was tired because the day started extremely early. I got to the hotel after 12 p.m. I rolled up to the front desk with my backpack and a large travel bag. I felt myself walking into a cool room. I could smell that familiar hotel scent. I could hear the humming of the air conditioner. I could feel the nice big double bed my body was about to sink into after a nice hot shower.

I stood there and stared at the agent when he told me I had to wait four hours for a room. The hotel had a party come in during the weekend and every room was booked. No amount of protesting could fix the situation. All I could do was wait. I flew in one day early to avoid the rush of the first day of residency. I learned from the first residency why this was a wise decision. I grabbed a seat in the waiting area and used my suitcase as a pillow to rest.

Every learner I met, whether they showed up early or after checkout, had to wait hours for a room. The limited cleaning staff had to clean each room. Some customers did not check out on time which made the wait longer. To make up for the inconvenience, the hotel manager gave me a card for "free" internet and "free" breakfast. I found out later those things were already free. The trick worked to keep everyone calm.

The manager was kind enough to secure my luggage. I went to the restaurant and indulged in one of the most delicious salads I had ever eaten. I met another learner in the same predicament as me but arrived even earlier. We sat at the table with her daughter and her grandson. We talked about where we came from, and our aspirations for the program.

After lunch I returned to the foyer which gave me a small view of the lobby; it was beautiful. As I mentioned before, I love the sound of water. Wherever I am in a place where water flows my spirit feels at peace. In the lobby was a huge three-tier fountain. The water was thunderous, and gorgeous luxurious plants surrounded it.

The learner who was in the restaurant with me finally was assigned a room. She told me if I needed to rest, I could join her in her room until my room was ready. I did not want to miss the first opportunity to get a room, so I stayed in the foyer. After four hours I was finally assigned a room. It was not what I expected, but it was clean.

The name did not match the odyssey I walked into. After being there for an hour, the toilet bowl would not flush. I had to make a phone call to the lobby to have someone fix it. A tall young lady came to troubleshoot the issue. She agreed that she had to replace the entire flushing mechanism.

I was fortunate with my room which I cannot say about others in my situation. The learner sitting in the restaurant had an extremely hard bed, another had a full-size mattress on top of a queen-sized box spring, another learner's bed broke and one learner had pubic hairs stuck to her shower wall. I went down to the lobby after 6 p.m. and there was another learner with a huge cart of luggage still waiting for a room. What can you do in a situation like that? Laugh, be grateful, meet wonderful people, learn, and then get home to your family.

My Second Residency

The next morning, I went downstairs for breakfast. I saw a learner looking for a place to sit and I invited her to sit with me at my table. We introduced ourselves and started a casual conversation. She told me how nice the people at the front desk were because they blessed her with a card so she could have "free" breakfast and internet during her stay. It almost broke my heart to tell it was a trick.

During the week we had the best professor who kept us entertained with magic tricks and the game of "Simon Says." It broke up some stress.

The second professor was a brilliant methodologist. A course in tactful communication would have done her well. They allowed each learner to sign up to have fifteen minutes to speak with them.

As I went up to the desk, the methodologist asked, "Is there a study that says you need to do this topic?"

I sheepishly answered, "No." I was confused by her question. She did not touch my paper, and she did not look at me.

She said, "Then you can't do the study."

I tried to explain that my first residency professors aligned my study, and they said it was fine. She insisted I could not do the study. I tried to bring up another issue to the other professor but each time I tried to say something the methodologist made a snarky remark as if I was not standing there. I was already upset and felt that I should walk away from the table before my fifteen minutes were up. I wanted to avoid a verbal confrontation at all cost. It would have been unpleasant for her and unproductive for me.

I returned to my seat and focused on my work. If there is nothing else that you take from this book, please remember what I told you about the gap or need statement for additional research. **If you do not have a gap or need, you cannot do the study!** It was three years and money wasted even after everything else was "aligned."

Residency days were always long. Class time could also be overwhelming. We worked diligently and focused on our assignments. Although the hotel suites were blah, the hotel did a wonderful job when it came to hospitality.

The staff fed us like kings and queens. Every evening after class the staff supplied free drinks for those who indulged in cocktails. It was the first time I felt like a "Dr." There was glassware, silverware, and delicious food for every meal. It was a far cry from my first residency. We had wonderful classrooms. There was a beautiful venue for the kids to play around, but the food was beyond interesting.

One feeling many of us had was overwhelming loneliness. Some of us broke down in tears. Every emotion you feel as a doctoral learner, are emotions other learners have felt. You might be feeling some negative emotions right now. With the right support, you will get through it. I told everyone at the residency I would cross the graduation stage and I would wear a white t-shirt, sneakers, and a pair of jeans when I did. It was my symbolic way to say I could finally relax after the stressful journey.

I met some of the most incredible people at my second residency who wanted to remain friends. I passed a sheet around the class to collect their names and email addresses and I created a board on social media. Some joined the group while others could not because of their occupations, and several were not interested.

Many of my cohort members are either gone from the program or graduated. I emailed everyone on the list in 2017 and only one person responded. She told me she graduated in 2016. I have no idea what happened to the others. Only a small number of my cohort members remained in the group I formed, and some do not comment. I considered shutting it down to focus on other things, but something always stops me as I feel connected to them having experienced the same things.

If during your journey you feel it is not for you, or you cannot continue, it is okay to stop. This path is not for everyone. I got to the point where I parked my bus. It was time for me to quit my journey.

Really Dark Days

When I got home I focused on the feedback from my methodologist. I also focused on the feedback the methodologist at the second residency had given. I received an A and was extremely pleased.

Despite the issue with my gap, I worked as hard as I could on the other assignments. How I wished we had a methodologist during my first residency. Though our methodologist was brash, she knew her stuff. The day after she told me I could not do my study, the professor told me to keep looking for an article. He said it is out there, and I would find it. I never did.

After months of trying to find an article to support my topic I fell in love with, I decided to have a permanent breakup. I never wanted to hear of it again. I started another class and was the last one standing. Everyone else was gone. Before the previous class ended, my cohort member told me his document got approved. Mine was not, but I was happy for him.

He mentioned he was dropping out. I begged him not too. He was the only learner who had not taken a break, and I felt he needed one. After not seeing him in class, I wrote to find out what happened, but he did not respond until months later. He told me that his document had been approved, but he saw the scam the school was running.

He never went into detail about what the scam was, but he had finally had enough, and he quit because of it. I had disdain for my chairperson, but my friend and the chairperson were like gasoline and fire.

In the previous class, my chairperson wrote on my iteration that I was the only one not progressing in the class. I was not progressing, but I was working extremely hard and doing what my chair told me to do when he gave me the little feedback he did. His comment made me feel bad. I worked myself into a frenzy to do better, but nothing worked. I discovered this chairperson said the same thing to the learner who left, and the one who had taken a short break.

In 2014 my life started to spiral. I started having leg problems from sitting behind a computer for hours every day at work. I sat for hours after work, and on weekends working on my document. The picture of me to the right is one of my favorites. Although I do not like taking pictures, I love this one. In this picture, you see a beautiful smile. What you do not see is the pain I was in. I was at home recuperating from a blood clot in my right leg. I could not  stand or walk for more than a few minutes. I had the picture taken from a seated position because I was in agony.

For months I had problems keeping my legs still. They would move constantly while I was laying down or sleeping. Over time my legs moved from twitching to a terrible unrelenting-burning sensation. My left leg always felt like it was on fire. At work, I would have to stand up to type because sitting made the pain and burning worse. I would have to go on walks during my breaks, stretch, and rub my legs. No amount of massaging made it feel better.

There was no medical doctor or local facility available to treat my medical condition which did not help things or my stress level. Once a month I drove out of town to see a specialist. A technician took sonograms of my legs. After a diagnosis of deep vein thrombosis, I made plans to correct the issue. I had to try some techniques for a month before my insurance company would approve my request for the medical procedures. I wanted the month to quickly pass. Nothing worked, and my medical condition was getting worse. I wanted the pain and burning to stop.

Warning: *The following paragraphs may be objectionable to some readers as they are medically explicit.*

I scheduled my first procedure. The specialist gave me some Ginkgo Biloba and a mild sedative to relax. He had a huge television-like monitor mounted onto the wall so I could see what he was doing. I was grateful everything was in a gray. I would not have been able to watch if it was in color. My left leg was more problematic than the right leg, so he started there.

He made a small incision on my left leg above my ankle bone which made the place where he would insert a long wire with a heat probe at the tip to thread through my vein. It took several minutes to get the tip of the wire through it. He threaded it up to my thigh. When the wire was all the way through the vein, he pulled it out very slowly. Every three or four inches he pressed a button. The button heated up the tip of the probe and burned the vein to collapse it.

He explained that once he burned the vein my body would absorb it and the good veins around it would take over the blood flow. It is amazing how our bodies work, and it was fascinating to be able to see a silhouette of this procedure.

There was no pain or discomfort during the procedure, but I was sore and in pain for weeks after it. My left leg gave me the most distress, but my right leg became a bigger problem. A month after the procedure on the left leg, the doctor did the same procedure on the right leg. Things went well with no issues. It was two weeks later, on a Thursday when things got bad.

I went to see my gynecologist and within twenty-four hours, things rapidly changed. I do not remember what I wanted to talk to my gynecologist about, but I do remember when he walked into the room, I said, "Dr. R, I'm fat!"

He started laughing and told me to eat four boiled eggs every morning to start losing weight. Four boiled eggs every morning was not something I was interested in doing. I love blazing-hot boiled eggs, but I could barely stand to eat two at one time, much less four.

My gynecologist had nothing to do with my leg. I remember this day as a reference because the next day everything went to hell. I went home and resumed my regular day. When I woke up the next day, I could not walk. It was the most unimaginable pain I have ever experienced. I felt like I had a Charlie horse on steroids.

I tried to take care of housework, but my leg made it impossible to complete any chores. Taking a shower became so painful I had to cut my normal shower time in half. I asked my son to rub my leg, but that did not help either. Only lying down with my leg elevated gave me any form of relief.

I hesitated about going to urgent care because I was scheduled to see my specialist the next day. After the long ride to the doctor's office, I strategized how to get from the waiting area into the room. I did not have crutches and there were no wheelchairs. When I got on the table, the technician did another sonogram. He called the specialist into the room.

As the specialist looked at the screen, he asked very calmly as he refrained from looking at me, "Who is your primary care doctor?"

After giving my doctor's name, I asked what was the matter? He said I had a blood clot. The tech told me as soon as he saw my leg, he knew the diagnosis. My leg looked normal to me, but the tech said it was red and swollen. He was not allowed to say anything.

The blood clot went from my ankle all the way up to my thigh in the exact area I had my procedure done a few weeks before. A scary aspect was, by asking my son to massage my leg it could have caused pieces of the clot to dislodge and travel through my body. I was off work for a month. My primary care doctor prescribed anticoagulants, and I had multiple tubes of blood drawn to rule out cancer. I had to see a hematologist. The hematologist checked my bloodwork to make sure everything was going well with the anticoagulant. I was grateful my bloodwork was fine.

Before my primary care doctor released me back to work, he gave me a list with strict instructions which required me to get up every two hours and walk for ten minutes. He told me to go immediately to the emergency room if I fell, bumped my head, or started to bleed. Considering I am a woman, I asked, "Bleeding from where?"

His response, "Anywhere," caught my attention and increased my level of stress.

I was grateful he provided his instructions in writing because I had a supervisor who was a tyrant. If I was not at the desk working, it was a huge ordeal. The letter assured me I would not have any issues at work. I was mindful not to take advantage of this reprieve. I knew how far I could go before I had to be back at my desk. Walking was what I needed; it made my legs feel better.

No one knew the seriousness of the medical condition with my leg. Recuperating was long and painful. You never realize how important a body part is until you experience issues with it. I needed to use my legs every day which made the healing process slower.

After every procedure, I wore compression stockings for two weeks. My legs were sore and swollen and I walked like Frankenstein for weeks until the swelling and soreness vanished.

Shoes in my closet would not fit my feet due to the swelling in them. My legs became sensitive to cold weather, and driving proved uncomfortable. Although only a few people knew of my medical condition, no one knew the depth of my pain because I kept it to myself with no way to fully describe it. The word pain does not even come close to describe what I felt.

A few months after I returned to work several of us were laid off. I lost my job right before Christmas. The specialist told me for months I had to quit my job because the constant sitting made my leg issues worse. I thought how easy it was for him to say that I had to quit my job. He was a doctor and had plenty of money. I, on the other hand, was not so fortunate. I refused to quit my much-needed job. In the end, I was glad I did not resign.

The layoff made the decision for me, but I did not walk away empty handed. The company gave me two weeks' notice and a small severance package. I was grateful for the years I worked for this company and the time off that I needed.

I could not afford to lose my job, but I made a habit of paying my bills and car note ahead of the due date. At the time of my layoff I had paid my car notes six months in advance which came as a small blessing. I was able to handle my bills for several months and I enjoyed the extra time at home with my family not having to worry about work deadlines after getting home. It was wonderful not to have to come home tired from work and take care of household duties.

I decided to go on a vacation in April of the next year. As I mentioned earlier, I decided to take better care of my body and I hired a personal trainer in 2015 when something happened. This event was pivotal in me parking my bus almost at the end of my journey.

While I worked, I suffered from deep depression. No one knew because I suffered in silence. I felt stuck and did not know what to do and realized I should have quit my job earlier. The truth is, I could not afford too. Likewise, I should have left school because I was not progressing but going deeper into debt. I was tired from working while going to school which added to my stress and to my depression.

There was a time in my life when I could not wait to go to work every day. I loved what I did for a living. I loved my first supervisor. With the exception of a few people, I adored my co-workers. It was a wonderful place to work, and I had so much fun! In 2014 going to work was not fun for me anymore. I was tired of having to sit behind a desk for hours while succumbing to pain and I was physically, and mentally drained.

The problems I had with my university was the root of my depression. No one from the university would help me while I sank deeper and deeper into debt with each course I took.

Working out with my trainer and losing weight took my mind off school. Since work was no longer an issue, I was able to get the rest I desperately needed. I felt good about the progress I made with my trainer, but I remained depressed.

One night I went to bed like any other night. Around 3 a.m. I heard a loud crash. I walked downstairs to find my favorite cup in large pieces on the floor. The way my favorite cup looked on the floor was symbolic of how I had felt for months. I thanked my cup for the years of joy it provided, cleaned the fragments, laid it to rest in the trash can with respect, and then went back to bed.

By 6:30 a.m., I was unable to take a full breath. I had the most horrible pain on the right side of my chest. I thought it was a broken rib or a sprain because my trainer worked me extra hard the day before.

The next day when my trainer arrived for my session, I explained there was no way I could work out. I knew my body, realized something was wrong, and I was in too much pain.

For the rest of the day I was in pain, but at least able to breathe. At night I experienced agony and could not take a full breath; it was too painful.

My ex-husband and I have no family outside of our children in the state we live in. We depend on each other in times of need. Over the years we cultivated an amicable friendship. Our friendship was full of love and respect, with the occasional "get out of my house!" He was someone I called my best friend and the one who found the specialist who treated my legs. We live close enough so our children could have access to both of us, but far enough to allow each other our privacy.

I let my ex-husband know how I was feeling and asked if he could bring me painkillers. The painkillers did little to ease the pain. I spent the entire weekend in bed trying to nurse myself back to health.

I could not eat so I asked if he would mind going to the store to buy me a healthy smoothie. The lady who made my smoothie was a new friend. I suspect my ex-husband told her I was sick. When I got the cup, the front of it was covered with hearts and a sad face.

The following Monday I went to the store to thank her. After explaining my symptoms, she said, "It sounds like you have a blood clot."

I said "Oh my goodness! I forgot I had a clot in my leg last year." I decided if I felt the same pain, I would go to the emergency room. That night, it happened again. I went to the emergency room and the triage nurse took my vital signs. I told her I was having difficulty breathing. She said it would be a two-hour wait because my vitals were perfect.

I told her I felt like I was going to faint. It did not matter; I had to wait for two hours. We made a call to another hospital. It had a two-hour wait too. There might have been a different outcome if I went to the other hospital, but I felt it would be a waste of time. I decided to leave. If I was going to pass out, I would do it in my home. Under the condition that I would go to the doctor the next day, my ex-husband took me home.

Early the next morning, I was in the doctor's office. My doctor had me take x-rays, ordered a urinalysis test, and bloodwork. She gave me medication for pneumonia. Later that afternoon, my doctor's nurse called. I had to report to the hospital for a magnetic resonance imaging (MRI). One of my blood tests came back elevated.

The quickest they could see me was the next day. My ex-husband and I made the forty-five-minute drive. When I got to the office, a nurse gave me an IV and led me in a room to have my MRI done. When I was lying on the table female technician told me to remain still. She told me I would feel like I was urinating on myself, but that would not be the case. I did not feel like I was urinating on myself, but everything felt uncomfortably warm.

I told the technician I needed to throw up. She said the feeling would pass, and it did. After the MRI, the technician told me to wait in another room. She told me the nurse would come in and remove the IV port after the doctor reviewed my images. When the nurse entered, I cheered. I could finally get this dreadful thing out of my arm and get back to the comfort of my home. She did not come anywhere near my port. She said, "Ma'am the doctor would like to speak with you, can you come into this other room?"

A feeling of dread flooded within me. A few minutes later the doctor came in and said, "Ma'am you can't go home. You have a blood clot in your lung."

I said, "What? Is it mild or moderate?"

He said, "It's moderate."

I broke down into tears and asked if they could bring my ex-husband into the room. When I told him what happened, he did not have much of a reaction. I do not consider a pulmonary embolism (PE) to be mild or moderate. What I meant to ask was if it was big or small. I do not know why I asked that question other than I must have been in shock. No matter the size, a PE can kill you.

I asked my ex-husband to call my sisters and let them know because I did not want to talk to anyone. I heard one of my sister's voice over the telephone, but I have no idea what she said to him.

The nurse called for hospital transportation. A man showed up with a wheelchair and we headed to the emergency room waiting area. I was bumped to be seen in front of everyone.

A triage nurse took me to a room and asked questions, and then she stepped out of the room for a few minutes. It was as if the entire emergency room came to a standstill. I was wheeled into a room with two doctors and two nurses. To make matters worse, I was in the middle of a shift change. It was organized chaos! I did not grasp the gravity of the situation. I did not see the images, and I did not want to think about things at the moment.

While the nurses worked on my IV bags, I had to make a quick decision on which anticoagulant I wanted to take. One doctor gave me a choice of three medications. Another doctor told me not to take the first one because it was a bad drug. I did not need his advice because I had heard about the drug before and I wanted no parts of it. The second drug was made from pork. I would have to give myself daily shots in my abdomen. The third was the more expensive medication I had taken before.

Do you remember what I said earlier about pain? Which one do you think I chose? I chose the medication I used when I had the blood clot in my leg. The medication was extremely expensive, but I only had to take one pill each morning. I did not have to check my blood or adjust my diet.

I cannot describe how I felt when the doctor told me I had a blood clot in my lung. Only people who experienced this know what it feels like. I was frightened to find out I had walked around with this interloper for days thinking I had broken a rib.

I knew how dangerous a PE diagnosis is for a person as I remembered having heard on the news about people who died suddenly from this condition. Death from this condition filled my mind. My doctor admitted me to the hospital, and I did not see outside for three days. Every morning without leaving my bed, I could see the horizon. Each new day I told God what a privilege it was to see such a beautiful sunrise.

My attending physician told me it would take at least two months for my lung to heal because it had been injured. She explained the mechanics of a PE. She said painkillers were the worst thing I could have taken as they could have thinned my blood and caused the clot to travel in my lung. She assured me if I stayed on my medication, I would be fine and would heal. I asked her if I could fly. Now more than ever I needed to go home. She said I could fly, but I had to be sure to take my medication.

With the diagnosis of a clot in my lung, it sent me through every kind of fear. It affected me psychologically, emotionally, and physically. I read up on PE and learned that one clot can turn into smaller ones once it goes into the lung. It was the first time I was terrified of getting sick and dying. I had never been hospitalized or subjected to hospital food outside of childbirth.

When I was released, I was afraid to sleep. I asked my ex-husband to spend the night and sleep next to me as close as possible. I was afraid if I died in my sleep our children would find me. It sounds overdramatic but if you have never been through something like this, it is difficult to understand. May you never find out what it feels like.

I was fortunate I did not lose my life. Every cough or shot of pain sent fear through my soul. Would this be my last cough? Did my blood clot move? It took a week before I felt safe to sleep alone.

Chores such as sweeping the floor and washing clothes sapped my strength. I could not take clothes from the washer and put them in the dryer without having difficulty breathing. I had to sit down, rest and catch my breath for at least thirty minutes before I could finish. I soon discovered that lifting my arms over my head while taking a shower to clean my armpits left me winded and tired too. I had a home to take care of, so I worked within my limits.

A week after my doctor released me from the hospital, I tried driving. Even that sapped my strength.

The last thing on my mind was working out. I did not have the strength or breath to do a single burpee, squat, pushup, or wall sit. I wondered if I would regain my full strength, but I did after eight months.

All of this time as I recovered from my PE episode, I still took classes. I did the best I could to keep up; but it was not my priority, saving my life became my only priority.

When I was hospitalized, I was on a seven-day break from class, which was a blessing. If I was in the coursework part of my program with no breaks, I would have had to take a leave of absence.

Two months later I went on my trip and had the time of my life. I had not seen my island home for over fourteen years and did not stop smiling until it was time to leave. The fresh air, culture, people, food, festivities, music, and sunshine were what I needed to heal me from within. I did not worry about school, about dying, and about being tired or out of breath because I was not. I made sure I took my medication as prescribed even though I felt better. The week went by fast and I was on my way back to my stateside home.

A few days after coming home, I had to deal with more stress from my chairperson. Now that I was the only learner in the class, I hoped things would get better. In fact, it got worse.

One night while in a deep sleep, I suddenly woke up with the first and only panic attack I have ever suffered. I do not remember if I was dreaming or if my mind wandered when panic enveloped me. I jumped out of bed and paced the floor. I freaked out because I had one class left that financial aid would pay for.

I had no idea how I was going to pay to finish the program or if I would. I was thousands of dollars in debt with nothing to show for it. Before I started, the university told me it would be a specific amount of time and money for the program. No one told me if I did not get out of the program at a specific point, financial aid would stop paying for classes. No one told me I would have to pay for the classes on my own if I wanted to finish the program.

I hired another editor who helped me choose my final topic. I let my chairperson know. He told me I had to have university permission to change it. I knew this was untrue, and I replied to his email and informed him I did not have to get approval from the university. He said he thought it was true because he had to do it for another student.

I did not address the issue anymore. I asked my counselor and the woman I sent my document to who would not help me. They told me it was not true. Even with this lie, they would not release me from this chairperson.

I continued to work on my document and paid close attention to the instructions. I recognized the same pattern I had seen before - a request to add more information. I stood my ground and told the chairperson I was within the guidelines of the instructions. I did not hear any more about it after my last email. I had no intentions of writing another sixty-plus page document and wasting another year, more time, or more money. I refused to add another word, and I meant it! I knew this would become a point of contention. He would never send my document forward. That is when I assessed everything that happened to me since he became my chairperson.

While dealing with my clot issue, I was so scared of losing my life I had forgotten about being depressed. Here it was revisiting me with a fury. I felt beaten, I had no tears left, and I did not care anymore. My PE incident showed me what things in my life were important.

After I was laid off, I was able to take my children to school and be there for them. I helped my son when he was not sure if he was cooking something right for his dad. I loved it when he asked me how to cook a dish or when he said, "Mom, I'm trying to fry this cornbread, but it keeps falling apart."

I never cooked fried cornbread before, but I could see the batter was fine. With a little adjustment to the heat, I turned over a perfect golden-brown cake. I reminded my son how to clean poultry, and meat with vinegar and water. Those were the things that were important.

After a day of contemplating, I decided it was time to quit the program. I wanted off this bus. I sent my counselor an email and asked her not to schedule any more classes until further notice. I could have sat out of my classes and gotten another committee. As far as I was concerned, it was time to move on. I wanted my life and my freedom back. I wrote my chairperson to tell him I was leaving. It was obvious that no matter what I did he had no desire to help me succeed.

Although my email was calm, I had lost all respect for him and his title. Instead of addressing him as Dr., I addressed him as Mr. He did not like that at all. He told me he was going to contact his supervisor to make a formal complaint. My response was "I cannot go against your free will, do what you have to do. God will make the crooked things straight." I could not find a smidgen of respect for this person and I did not care how he felt.

He had no idea of the private hell he sent me or my other cohort members through. He had no idea about my illness, the sleepless nights, the days I cried until I ran out of tears, the deep sinking levels of depression I suffered at his hands, the thousands of dollars of mine he wasted, my concern about money to pay for the rest of my program, the money I would have to pay back due to his incompetence, and the fact that I would walk away with nothing.

The university backed him and there was nothing I could do about it. When I tried to call him Dr., my tongue could not move. I was wrong for calling him Mr. His title was important to him. He bragged constantly about his accomplishments. I did not respect the man, but I should have had respect for his title.

I was not allowed to contact my methodologist. I knew other learners who contacted theirs and pure wrath came down on them because of it. I was not concerned about wrath; I was leaving. My methodologist would not care if I left or not. I felt a strong urging on the inside that would not allow me to leave until I thanked her for the feedback on my document although it was many months before.

When I sent the email, I told her although I could have been angry over her feedback, I knew favor when I saw it. For me to have gotten angry would have been foolhardy. The document was a disaster. Her feedback was full of compassion and her questions triggered my brain to think. I finally understood what I was supposed to do. It was the opposite of everything my chairperson instructed me.

I told her if she had been my chairperson I would have been finished already. I let her know I was leaving, and I wanted to say thank you before I left. My methodologist replied to my email. I was surprised her response was calm and unladen with a stern warning not to contact her again.

She mentioned she was thinking about me right before she received my email. That was the end of the conversation, and I closed the door. It hurt to think about quitting, but it was time. My personal goal was to always finish whatever I started. My program was no different. I had a history of starting things, but once the novelty wore off, I would move on to a new adventure. There was a void in my life because of it. I was not that person anymore. God redeemed the time on some unfinished business in my life. I took the opportunity and finished them.

I decided to never turn down any opportunities and to do something every year that scared me. I am not saying I am going to run over a mile-long hot bed of coals barefooted with gasoline on my legs. I am "old" and "ugly" for a reason. I just love things that challenge me. It is the reason I decided to face my fear of heights by jumping out of a plane in 2014. Side note, there are some things in this world you should only do once. I will leave it at that.

Between 2015 and 2016 I had no need for daredevil tactics. My blood clots had given me the fright of my life and my determination to get cured was enough for me. I learned a valuable lesson by leaving school. I realized that some of my motivation to stay in my program was to stop my chairperson from getting satisfaction. It became a game of wits between us. One learner already quit with no idea of what happened to the two others. I was not going to allow him to force me out. My focus was not where it was supposed to be. I did not care about it anymore.

I learned just because you've started something, does not mean that you will finish. We need to stop being so hard on ourselves when we fail. I was notorious for being my worst critic. When I failed at anything, it hurt me to my soul. The negative things that were drummed into my head as a child would come back to taunt me. I have been freed from that. The failure is not in trying and failing. The failure is in not trying at all. Failure has its purpose and some things are just not meant to be.

You must know when to start something when to keep trying, and you must learn when to walk away. It is better to take an opportunity and fail than not try and then live with regret. You also cannot casually start things and quit when you become bored or when it gets hard. You will have an unfulfilled life with zero accomplishments and plenty of regrets you do not want. Regret is an awful emotion to live with.

I wanted to earn my Ed. D., I failed, but at least I tried. I tried until I could not try anymore. I was proud of it. I would not be digging myself into any more debt and I felt at peace with my decision. If you are ready to leave your journey behind, do not make the decision until you are calm and have found your peace. When you make decisions in the moment of passion, it is usually the wrong one. If you decide to take a break, go back when you say you will.

The next day after I quit my program, I received an email from the woman who refused to help me. My first urge was to hit the delete button, but I read it. My methodologist contacted someone and asked if she could become my chairperson. Someone else would replace her role. I had no idea a committee member could change roles, but it happened to me.

I had to read the email several times before I believed it. Out of all committee members, the methodologist was the least favorite. This was the person who decides if your documents get approved or rejected and they are notorious for being difficult. What if I had gotten angry at my methodologist and said some unkind words instead of thanking her? Another lesson learned – always be respectful in your replies even if you are so angry you want to bite the lid off a can.

After I read the email a couple more times, I replied with a "YES!" I found my fire and motivation again. My new chairperson told me about her expectations. She was no pushover, but she was patient and supportive. When I sent my first iteration, I asked her what the problem was with my citations that the previous chairperson kept sending back.

She commented on the document that he could have told me what the issue was a long time ago. Citations should be in alphabetical order. Well, who does not know that? I looked at the block of in-text citations and there it was -- one name out of alphabetical order. I should have paid more attention to what I wrote which may have prevented the back and forth with my document, but when you keep looking at the same document over and over, there are things you will not see. Trust me when I tell you this.

When I read her comment and found my mistake, I thought of my ex-chairperson. My blood boiled with the fury of a scorned woman. I thought of the weeks my ungraded document went back and forth and the money I had wasted. What would it have taken for him to say what my new chairperson said? I quickly got past my anger. I reminded myself that I was on the uprise, and I would never have to work with him again.

With my new and wonderful committee in place, there were days of frustration. The process was lengthy, but I was grateful. I was grateful because I was progressing.

When Murphy's Law and
Data Collection Shake Hands

I decided to talk about data collection in this book because my experience was not what I expected. I wish someone had warned me, so I am warning you. This is the part of your journey where you will be excited and have the most fun. I wanted learners to be aware of the emotional side of research. Things may not always go as planned.

Go into your data collection with no expectations and with an open mind. Keep focused even if an interview makes you want to fall asleep. Give your participant your undivided attention. My study was qualitative, so some of this information may not pertain to you. I hope you enjoy reading it and decide to do a qualitative study one day if you have not.

If you are conducting a qualitative study, you may want to create your own instruments as I did. Instruments are things like a demographic questionnaire or a list of interview questions needed to collect your data. After I created my instruments, I had to field test them.

There were a lot of issues with my interview questions during field testing. The first mistake I made was not having enough questions to meet the minimum requirements for my interviews. Another issue was my dictation programs. They did not work well, and I had to discard them. I would have made a fool of myself had I not tested them. Check with your university to see if you must conduct a field test. Having an expert panel critique your instruments may suffice. Even if these options are not required, find three or four experts, preferably with doctorates to review your questions.

Decide how you will protect the identity of your participants. I do not recommend the use of pseudonyms. Imagine someone who conducted a study in my city and gave one of the participants my name as a pseudonym. What if the research-study was something bizarre, and my boss happened to read it? What would stop my employer from thinking it was me? My name, location, and identity were not protected even though I had nothing to do with the study. You must always protect your participants.

I encourage learners to use letters, numbers, or a combination of both. You can also list them as participant 1, etc. How you choose to use them is up to you. I love butterflies. They work hard to transform from one stage to the other. I love how they show off their beautiful colors once they appear from their uncomfortable abode. Yellow butterflies remind me of home. I remember how they made me feel when I was a child. If I can get away with it, I use them as my love symbol in everything I do.

To Identify my participants, I chose the letter B and a number to wink at them. Every time they use a screen reader and hear the letter B with their assigned number, they know I am sending them love. You can pick whatever resonates with you.

Create a demographics questionnaire as race, age, and gender can influence the results of your study and create a need for more research. When you create your questionnaire, insert a logic. A logic is a criterion that will kick a potential participant out of your questionnaire. No one will know it is there but you.

My study was on the blind or visually impaired. If my potential participant recorded that they were not blind or visually impaired, the logic would have kicked them out of the questionnaire.

Be careful who you send your information too and double check email addresses and phone numbers.

Another question that should have a logic is permission to audio record the interview. If your potential participant does not give permission to audio record, kick them out of your study.

Some professors or researchers may not agree with this, but unless you know shorthand or have the skills of a stenographer, you will not be able to capture every word by writing a participant's response. You must have clear and detailed audio recordings to properly code your transcripts. After I listened to my audio recordings, I could not believe how much information I had forgotten or did not hear at all. Your chair might request a copy of your transcripts. If you do not have enough data, they will tell you to go back and collect more. That is the last thing you will want to do.

When you create your interview questions, make sure the questions are open-ended by starting each question with, "Can you tell me…" You want your participants to answer without leading them. Construct questions so they address your gap statement, purpose, problem statement, and answer your research questions. Never ask offensive or personal questions and always put "decline to answer" as a choice for an answer on your questionnaire as it puts less stress on your participant to respond to your questions. If you feel the question should be answered, you may add a logic to it.

With my new committee members in place, things progressed quickly although it was not easy. My documents were approved from the second stage to the Institutional Review Board (IRB) within a year and a half. I was now in my fourth year of an advertised and promised three-year program.

I had wonderful support from my new committee. I was able to learn and help others while I struggled through my program. My topic was unique and by being unique it took a bit of time to get through IRB. I also made several mistakes when I completed my application.

I conducted a mock interview, field tested and had my recruitment letter ready. Finally! After two months I received approval to conduct research (data collection)! **Never recruit or conduct data collection**

before IRB approval. What you can do is to contact organizations you want to work with.

Find out what you have to do to get permission to conduct research with them. If they decline, keep driving your bus. When you get approval to recruit, do not contact potential participants. Get a liaison in the organization to do it for you.

When I first approached the organization for permission to conduct research, my liaison was excited because they needed the study. In my mind, I knew potential participants would be ready to jump on board since the liaison was so excited. Yeah, right! It took over two weeks for anyone to come forward. Some were offended by one word in my topic sentence.

I was concerned about using the word and brought it up to my chairperson. She gave her rationale for why the word was right. I asked my son if he was offended by the word, he said, "No." I knew my study would not go forward if I did not relent. I did not like it, but I had to deal with it. Some fights you will not win. Get back in your seat, tighten your seat belt, check your mirrors, and drive your bus.

After explaining to my liaison why the topic was written the way it was, things started moving again. I conducted interviews and drove many miles to get to most of them.

For the first interview, I drove two hours one-way. Since I had my trusty cell phone and car charger, I did not print any directions. This was an enormous mistake. My phone worked great and found the destination with no problem. The trip home did not go as well.

Ten minutes after starting my return trip, the navigation on the phone quit working. I decided to take a random turn, and I ended up on a detour. A trip that should have taken two hours turned into four. Instead of stopping in a strange area with no stores, I decided to drive until I found a familiar exit. When I got home, I was hungry with a terrible headache, but I did not care. I had my first interview, and it went well. The other interviews were in a different direction but not a two-hour drive. At least they were not supposed to be.

The next block of interviews was a few days later. I scheduled three interviews in one day and walked with printed directions, but I still got lost.

When Murphy's Law and Data Collection Shake Hands

Two interviews lasted close to four hours when each was supposed to be sixty to ninety minutes. Some people have a lot to say and you should listen.

I planned to stop and pick up something for lunch but due to the extended time, I was unable to. I had to contact my last interview for the day and ask for their directions. While trying to find the address, a phone call came in from another participant to schedule another interview.

I was told if I did not get the interview done by the next day, I would not be able to obtain it. This participant was going out of town and would not be back before my deadline. I thought about squeezing in the interview, then decided against it. I was falling behind and had no clue how long the next interview would take.

I was physically exhausted, but I needed the interview and I was willing to drive back the next day. I scheduled the interview for the next morning and drove to my third interview. By the time I finished the third interview, it was dark, rainy, and cold.

On my way home, my phone decided to quit working again. I thought it was the app, so I found another one. It kept going out. I had no idea where I was, and I refused to stop to eat. It would have been wise to stop, but I wanted to get back to a familiar territory before the weather got worse.

I drove until I found a coffee shop where I could ask for directions to the freeway. It took so long to get to there, I thought I had missed it. I called my son for directions, but instead of helping, he asked why I had not downloaded an app. Frankly, I never heard of it. In aggravation, I said goodbye and continued to drive. I knew at that moment Murphy's Law and my data collection had shaken hands, and said, "Let's get her!"

My mind settled when I found the freeway. I started to reflect during the hour-long ride. I had experienced an eight-hour long day of extended interviews and being lost did not help. I was supposed to get to my destination, conduct my interviews in the required time, have something to eat, and get home during daylight. I could not wait to get in the shower, have something to eat, and go to bed.

My first interview participant said something which triggered an emotional switch in me. It was a statement made when I asked a question before getting set up for my interview. The answer to the question was innocent, but one that I the mother of a blind child had never heard before. My participant had no idea she said anything upsetting. I did not know she said anything upsetting until I was driving home.

The comment and interview area made me understand how much I took electricity and my vision for granted. On the way home, my mind took me back to the statement. I started to cry and did not stop for two days for more than one hour at a time. When I arrived home, I was cold, wet, and very hungry.

I took a shower and cried. I ate something and cried, I called my sister, and cried. I called my ex-husband to let him know I had made it home and cried. I told him I had to go back for another interview the next day and cried. I told him I was exhausted and cried. He offered to drive me the next morning, I cried. I went to bed and cried. I woke up the next morning and cried. I took another shower and cried. I got dressed and cried. I ate breakfast and cried.

I could have woken up, called my ex-husband, told him I was fine, say thanks for the offer to drive, go ahead and enjoy your day. I could have gone to my interview like any other day. That morning I could not do it. Thinking about driving that distance sucked what little energy which remained inside me. If I had tried to drive to obtain that interview it would not have only been selfish of me, but dangerous.

It took us an hour to get to my destination, and I cried the entire trip. I stopped crying when we got to the parking lot. I put on my stealth shoes so I could find my participant's home without my ex-husband knowing where I was going. Halfway through the interview, my participant broke down in tears. I had to stop the interview for a moment and pause the recording.

If your participant breaks down, reassure them that everything will be okay. Stop recording until they are ready to continue. If they cannot continue, reschedule the interview. Remember your audio recording will be sent to transcribers or anyone who has the right to listen to them. You want to protect their integrity. If they must cry, let them do so in private and never cry in front of your participant.

One interview had me laughing so hard I had to remind myself of my inappropriate behavior. We had such a wonderful interview. My participant told me if I ever came to the area, they had an extra bed if I needed a place to stay.

After data collection, it took me five days to consider picking up a pen to write anything. I wanted my brain to shut off, and I wanted to stop crying. I sent my audio recordings to a transcriptionist. She told me she had a box of tissues next to her. She had been crying while listening to the interviews. The statement that made me emotional was not recorded. The participant made it before I was set up for the interview. What I heard in some of those interviews were gut-wrenching stories. Many of the answers were things I had not asked, but things my participant shared, anyway.

Some of you might wonder what my participant said that made me emotional. I tussled whether I should put it in the book. Although it was not a part of the interview, it was an innocent discussion between two people. I do not know if any of you would understand or appreciate why it affected me. Though I shared the comment with the people who I chose to cry in front of, I never told my participant about the statement and I choose not to reveal it here.

I learned a lot from the mistakes I made when I collected my data. Though I had a blind child and used blind or visually impaired participants, I realized that I was the one who was blind. I was living in a bubble.

For some of you, your data collection will go awry. When I conducted my field test, I did it wrong, but it was nothing drastic. Until you understand research, you will make mistakes. For instance, you have your participants ready and at the last minute, one may decide they want nothing to do with you or your research. Remember, you told them they could leave any time they chose.

What do you do if this happens to you? Write it up as a limitation.

You can also recommend additional research to your study if it skews your data collection and results. Tell your reader why you recommend additional research and share the benefits. The wonderful thing about research is no matter how badly things go with your data collection, nothing is ever wasted. Your limitations will stop someone from making the same mistake.

If a participant drops out of your data collection and it leaves you without the minimum number of participants needed, you will have to continue recruiting until you meet the requirement. When you recruit, adhere to my advice and obtain about five participants above the minimum number of participants you are required to have for attrition. If potential participants or participants decide to opt out, it will be all right as long as you have the minimum number of participants you need.

I did not have that choice. I barely obtained the minimum I needed because of the word that offended so many. As a result, I had to hold on to every participant. That was the reason I went back for my interview when I was so tired.

Give yourself plenty of time to complete your recruitment and data collection. You have a year to conduct your research. A month should be enough time to recruit and collect your data after IRB approval. I had to change my start date while waiting for their approval. I conducted my last interview on the last day I had to collect data. The two-week delay could have been a huge ordeal If I did not carefully schedule my interviews.

You never know what is going to happen during data collection. Never conduct more than three interviews a day. It does not matter if interviews are on the telephone or during a video conference. Conducting interviews can drain your brain and body. If you have a participant that you must constantly prompt for responses, it will make you tired. If an interview ends before the required time, you will have to find a way to extend it. Prompt your participant by using the answers they provided.

My last interview was difficult. I had to discard sections of my questions, and the interview ended fifteen minutes early. I had to use answers to extend it.

If a participant asks you to repeat a question, you can either repeat it or rephrase it. Some participants might talk and not want to stop or might not talk much at all. Others might answer the question quickly while another might answer the question and not say anything else until you ask the next question. If this happens to you, never show your frustration.

Always have a pen and notebook. Although your participant should have your full attention; your participant may say things you will want to probe after they answer your questions. Let them know you will be taking notes while they answer your questions, and you will try not to interrupt them until they are finished answering.

Secure all notes or scrap paper along with your instruments for the allotted time required by the IRB.

Always leave home early. Never schedule interviews close together; you will need a break. Tell your participant they can take a break at any time. Take a printed copy of directions and always have phone numbers of your participants in case you get lost. We depend too much on modern technology.

Walk with breakfast, lunch, or dinner. Though I had a debit card and cash, it did no good.

I would not stop on any dark back roads. My phone had never given me any problems before, but it chose my data collection time to become outdated, and my children gave me a new one for Christmas that year.

Have no preconceived ideas of what will happen. Have a lot of fun and enjoy the experience. You are almost at the end of your journey.

After my data collection, I vowed I would never use the word that offended my participants in any research again. What can go wrong might go wrong or Murphy's law might say, "Let's give them a break?" All you can do is go with the flow.

Data Analysis

After data collection, you will have to analyze your data. To do this, you will have to transcribe your audio recordings. You can pay a transcriptionist to do it or you can do it on your own. There is a free data transcription program on the internet. You can upload your audio, set the rate of speed, re-loop your recordings according to your settings, and transcribe your data. After I conducted my field test interviews, this program was a game changer for me.

It was easy to use, and I had the choice of paying a small fee for a year's subscription. When it came to data collection, I needed to hire a professional. Ten participants produced over nineteen hours of audio. When I tried to transcribe them, it took half an hour to transcribe one page. When my transcriptionist finished what I started, I had two hundred and forty-four pages of Times New Roman, 12-point, single-spaced transcripts.

If you choose to hire a transcriptionist, ask if they are willing to sign a letter of confidentiality. A reputable transcriptionist will gladly sign it, and many will give you their contract for you to sign. There are websites that offer good transcriptionist for a decent price. Always ask if they charge by the word, by the page, by the minute, or by the hour and how long it will take to get your documents back.

After your data has been transcribed, listen to your recordings while you read your transcripts. This will allow you to catch any words your transcriptionist missed. No matter how long they have been transcribing, they are going to miss words. Some websites will display a percentage of accuracy on their site. If you listen and hear words that were written down as [inaudible], write them on the transcript.

After you review your transcripts, you can start to code your data. The more information you capture, the better your coding and the results will be. You can either hand code, use a data analysis program or both. My chairperson told me to hand code my data and boy, did I hate it. It is a wonderful skill if it is all you have access to, but I found hand coding to be double work. My reviewer told me, even if I hand coded, I had to use a data analysis program because hand coding does not capture everything.

I saw better results with the program than with hand coding. If your university allows you to hand code without using another program, hand code if you are proficient. If you must use a program after hand coding, skip hand coding and use a program. The program you choose will give better results if you effectively use it.

Themes you get from your data analysis will help fill in your gap or need by answering your research questions. When you answer your research questions, you will get your results. You will also address your problem statement and your purpose statement. Use your research skills to understand hand coding.

For those of you who decide to hand code, here are some tips I used. Hand code when you are relaxed and refreshed. I found mornings after taking a shower and having something to eat was the best time.

Coding, whether by hand or a data analysis program can take hours to days. Get two different colored highlighters. Use one for the question, and one to code words or phrases. Looks for words or phrases that keep reappearing in your data, or words or phrases you feel are relevant to your study. Read each sentence several times to find other words that might appear.

Open a new document and copy and paste the question, words, or phrases in a numbered list. Put the page and ID information of your participant on your sheet. The page number will allow you to have an easy reference to the transcript. The numbered list will give you the order you found each word or phrase. If you have to go back to the transcript and reread it, you can find these items easily. The ID will let you know which participant the information came from.

Read each word or phrase carefully. Write the theme you feel each item should fall under at the end of the sentence and circle it. If you find that some items you chose did not show up often or do not relate to your study, discard them.

If you decide to use a data analysis program, do some research on which would be best for you to use. You can do it on your own or hire someone to do it for you. Be aware that hiring someone to analyze your data will be expensive. Some learners use this option because it is time-consuming and difficult to do. If you analyze your own data or work with a tutor, you will be able to explain to your readers everything you did to code your data, and how you got your results. I encourage everyone to do their own data analysis.

My chairperson told me I had to code my data so I could write Chapter 4 detailing everything I did. I can write this section with ease to help you because of it. I did not have the money to hire a professional; so, I was forced to learn how to use a program on my own. I am grateful today for that hardship. Learning the program was difficult, but fun. When I found my themes and results, I felt a sense of excitement I would not have found if someone else did it for me. You do not have to hand code the way I did. Find your own system and work with that.

Whether you hand code or use a data analysis program you are going to need a codebook. The codebook should be the last step after you have chosen your themes. Find a site on the internet that can tutor you on how to create one. If you choose to create your codebook by hand, you can do it any way you choose. There is no right or wrong way to create one so have fun while doing it.

Data Analysis

If you are conducting a quantitative study, use a data analysis program, a statistician or both to ensure your data is analyzed correctly. Your data analysis whether qualitative or quantitative will be addressed in Chapters 4 and 5 of your dissertation.

Death of My Dearest Cohort

During my journey, I endured life-changing health issues that seemed to come out of nowhere. I worked so hard I was invited to join an honor society. I had no idea there was an honor society at the doctoral level. I did not want to get thrown out of my program, so I worked ridiculously hard. After checking it through the university, I accepted the membership.

My closest cohort and I lived in the same city. We connected when I put out a request on our university website to form a support group in my area. For four years we were a constant source of support. I never met him in person or spoke to him on the telephone. We played tag while going through our journey. When we became friends, he was ahead of me. Later, I got in front of him. I think I motivated him because once he got in front, he was out there.

We became friends on social media, and he gave me his telephone number. Still, we never spoke on the telephone or made plans to meet. I found out he made it into the honor society too. I was happy for him, but he was ecstatic. The induction ceremony was scheduled for a few months later. I had no plans to go because it was in another state. On the day of the ceremony, I contacted him through social media and asked if he went to the ceremony. He said he did not go either.

Death of My Dearest Cohort

Two or three weeks later I was on the social media site again. I saw a post on my feed from an old choir member. He posted to let someone else know that my dear friend, my cohort, had passed that morning. I refused to believe it. I did not know what to do with myself. After my initial shock, I got myself together and went on the internet to see if I could find a phone number for his wife.

I sent a message through her social media account with my condolences. I found a number and dialed it. I did not get in touch with his wife, but with his ex-wife. She was one of the sweetest people I have ever met. I introduced myself and explained how I met her ex-husband. After she told me what happened to my friend, she asked if I would write a letter to his homegoing (funeral). I was glad to do it and I shared a copy of an article he wrote for the university.

I do not like funerals, homegoings, or the topic of death. It is a debt we all owe and must pay, but I try to avoid the topic. If it were possible to choose my passing, I would tell everyone around me how much I loved them, I would give everyone hugs and kisses. I would tell them that I will see you on the other side, and with deuces up, say farewell in 3,2,1, *POOF.* Despite my feelings about death, I had to pay my respects to him.

My daughter offered to attend her first homegoing service with me. She told me before we went, she did not want to go up to the casket. When we went inside the funeral home, it was full. I found his ex-wife and their children. They greeted me with deep appreciation and introduced me as "the lady who wrote the nice letter for daddy." His ex-wife was even more of a lovely person that I thought once I met her.

I got in line to express my condolences to his wife, but she had to be taken outside. In truth, I tried to delay going up to the casket. This man was my friend and support for four years. This was the first time I was meeting him, and he was laying in a casket.

I walked up to the casket and stared. After saying goodbye and thank you, and after a long wait, they called us together for the service to begin. It was a beautiful farewell. The next day was the larger homegoing. From the reports I read, there were over five hundred people who went to pay their final respects to him. Going to his memorial service made me understand why we were friends for so long even without meeting in person.

My friend's death added grief, a brand-new round of depression, and fear. I asked God, "How could this happen? He worked so hard." He was so close to finishing, and he had a strong love for God. It seemed so unfair. I was afraid I was going to die when I dealt with my PE, but this feeling was different.

My friend was in the final stage of his dissertation process. He was weeks away from his final defense. He woke up on a Saturday like every other day, and a heart attack took him away from many people who loved him. A few weeks earlier we were two "old" folks inducted into an honor society of a doctoral program. I could not understand how something like this could happen.

We were too busy being happy. Although I had quite a way to go, I looked forward to calling my friend Dr. This was the second learner I heard about passing while going through this process. Both were from heart issues and that frightened me. Knowing who this wonderful man was, he would not have wanted me to feel the way I did.

I was in this program for almost six years. It was enough, and I wanted to get out. I sent a message to my committee members. I promised if they got my document back quickly, I would work as fast as I could to get it back to them. I was very honest and explained that I was feeling fear after the death of my friend.

We take so much for granted. What sense did it make for us to be friends for four years, live in the same small city and never meet in person or speak on the telephone? I talked to my daughter the night after the homegoing. I told her to make sure if she meets someone she cares about and considered them as a friend, to always listen to their voice. I never heard my friend's voice.

I have cohort members I keep in contact with on the telephone. Some are still going through the program. Some are no longer in the program, and some are trying to save money to finish. Show your friends respect and talk to them. Do not text or send instant messages every time you communicate. You never know what might happen.

I wrote my friend's name in my acknowledgment letter. I contacted his ex-wife to ask if she would accept a copy of this letter to share with his children and family. She was happy about this. We met in a coffee shop and she gave me a beautiful graduation card. She explained in deeper detail what happened to my dear friend. I was happy to hear he got a chance to speak to his children before he took his last breath. There was peace in that tiny detail.

I told his ex-wife that I wanted his name in my dissertation. With his hard work, persistence, love of writing, and kindness towards me, he deserved to have his name in someone's dissertation. I hoped it would bring his children peace.

I never received a reply from my friend's wife. Three days after he died and in the middle of his friend's posting their condolences, she abruptly shut down his social media account. I pray that she is healing quickly.

The Finish Line

Getting from data analysis to the dean's desk took another year. The end of my program was a long arduous process. My chairperson and I frequently chatted via a video conference and we enjoyed our conversations. Every meeting with her was fun. Sometimes we talked for hours about class and at other times we talked about anything else we wanted to discuss. Sometimes we did not care how jacked up we looked. On defense day, we both looked beautiful.

I was nervous that morning but ready to put this chapter in the journey of my life behind me. Everything was going well until I heard the familiar "ding dong" to let me know someone came in the virtual room. After my last committee member came in, I felt a wave of emotions. I could not believe this day had finally come. I started my program in 2012. I cried before, during, and after my dissertation defense and became Dr. Davis on October 19, 2017, at 11:00 a.m. This was my daredevil feat for the year.

While going through my program, I said I was not going to the graduation ceremony. I was angry! I was full of hate! I was bitter! I refused to be used as a pawn! I wanted no part of advertising this university! Unexpectedly, I was invited to attend graduation in an earlier class than I was supposed to.

Over the years family members and friends told me as hard as I worked, I should attend the graduation ceremony. A dear friend told me to forgive and go because even if I did not go, the graduation ceremony was still going to happen. It was not until I heard God speak to me that I decided to attend. I bought my regalia and searched for hotels.

This was my final graduation, and I wanted to be surrounded by my family. This was their graduation as much as it was mine. I wanted my ex-husband to be there too. He helped me when I was sick and struggling. He is family, and he deserved to be there. I did not know if he was going to accept my invitation to attend. I did not expect him too, but I asked, and he accepted.

While making reservations we discussed being on the same flight. I am an island girl and it is normal for island people to say we should split up the flights. If the plane crashed, our entire family would be gone. I do not live my life by old wives' tales or superstitions. I do have respect for them because they came from somewhere and the thought of us being on the same flight did cross my mind. I like to be positive, so I made my reservation.

When I made it, I was sure to ask what time the flight got in. I did not want a repeat of my second residency. I booked my hotel reservation with adjoining rooms and a minivan for transportation.

We had a late afternoon flight, but our day started incredibly early. Before we left, I asked everyone if they drank their orange juice and they said, "Yes." When I was a little girl, my grandmother told me to never get on a plane without drinking orange juice because it settles your stomach. Only one day in my life did I forgo that warning, and it did not end well.

The first time I flew with my daughter she was four or five years old. I had no juice in the house and no time to stop to buy any. I decided to wait for the drink service to order some. We got settled into our seats and prepared for takeoff. The second the plane moved my daughter looked at me with a strange expression. I asked if she had to throw up, she shook her head. I grabbed the bag from the seat in front of me. As my daughter buried her head into the bag and started throwing up, the smell hit me, and I had to grab a bag too. I looked at her and said, "In all the years I have been flying, I had never thrown up on a plane." I guess she felt better. She looked at me and smiled.

We got to the airport, boarded, and took our seats. This was the first commercial flight for my blind son and his second trip flying. His first trip was a four-seater, but he always wanted to have the commercial flight experience. Our family was spread out all over the plane.

I stood up to see where the other members of my entourage sat. My son sat in the middle of two strangers. I was surprised his dad had not insisted they sit together. I mentioned my son to this lovely stranger who sat next to me and she exchanged seats with him. She had a disabled child and understood. I thanked her deeply, and my son and I sat together.

I described with anticipation every sound and move. My son threw his hands in the air as you would on a roller coaster on take-off. From the moment wheels went up I knew it would be interesting. At the window sat a lovely and talkative woman. I was grateful to her because she was a welcome distraction. The flight was one of the most unsettling flights I had ever had, and it was my first flight on this airline. It was as if the pilots hit every air pocket they could find. I was so nauseated I thought one more bump would have done it and I started doubting Granny's advice.

I pulled out an almost finished roll of antacid that I threw into my backpack and popped two in my mouth. After the flight was over; I had made a new friend, and we exchanged information. I asked my son how he liked the flight. He thought it was great. As I described my experience, he said the turbulence was the best part. Go figure!

When we arrived at the hotel, the people at the front desk greeted me by name. I was impressed with this attention to detail. We walked into our rooms and relaxed for a bit. I had the taste for some hot wings, so I called downstairs to ask what restaurants sold them. They gave me the choice between a pub and the hotel restaurant. We decided to go downstairs and enjoy a nice dinner. After we returned to the room, I took my shower and went to bed while the youngsters went to check out the amenities of our hotel.

The next morning was an early wake-up for us all. I was tired but excited. We were running behind so we stopped at a drive-thru for breakfast.

When we arrived at the university, parking was easy to find. There was a short shuttle ride from the parking lot to the venue.

After going through security, I picked up tickets for everyone. I went upstairs, and my family stood around the lobby area before going into the auditorium. I checked in to receive my name card and was directed to the back of a long hallway. I was surprised at how organized the preparation area seemed. This was a far cry from the program. I signed in and received my regalia. After I got help with zipping my robe, I put my graduation tam on.

It is hard to describe that feeling. I felt like I was being crowned. When I walked down those stairs, I had the biggest smile on my face. My daughter waited at the bottom for me. The others left to find good seats, and she came to show me which side of the venue they chose to sit. I proudly walked into the auditorium and it looked huge. It looked bigger than the first time I saw it years before.

I saw an older woman dressed in her doctoral regalia. I do not know if she was graduating in my class or a faculty member. I stopped walking and told my daughter to give me a minute. I stepped out of the aisle, trying to squeeze back my tears. My daughter rested her hand on my shoulder and said, "Mom you earned it."

After I wiped away my tears, I went up front to an empty seat. A woman asked me for my name, told me how to hold my hood, and what to do once I got on stage.

When I got myself settled into my seat, I thought of my friend who passed. I looked toward the heavens, and whispered to him, "I had made it."

After waiting for an hour, the commencement ceremony began. We had an exciting speaker. After his speech, another short speech was given by the provost about earning a degree at our level.

We were asked to stand for recognition. I prayed to my heavenly Father that I would not trip going up the stairs after I was shuffled in front of a photographer to take my first picture. I strutted up the stairs without tripping, knowing the beautiful butterfly I became from this journey. I gave the announcer my name card, I was introduced, hooded, and quickly shuffled off stage. I have never taken so many pictures in one place before. There were two photographers off stage, and two photographers on stage. There was another photographer upstairs before the ceremony began. Every spot we had to stop for pictures were clearly marked with paper footprints. No one had to ask us to smile; once we started smiling, no one stopped.

I crossed the stage on April 28th, 2018 at 10:10 a.m., almost six years after I started my program. After our moment in the spotlight, we went back to our seats to wait for the other graduates to be recognized.

We were asked to stay behind until the entire auditorium emptied. They wanted all new doctors to take a group picture. After the group picture, I took pictures in the lobby and went upstairs to return my regalia. I noticed something when I was walking up the stairs. People were stepping out of my way and addressing me as "Dr." I did not notice it before the ceremony and chuckled beneath my breath because to me, I was still me.

Everything about graduation was surreal. Although I was there and had been conferred, I was still in that "I can't believe I am here" moment. I intended to enjoy every second of it.

After the ceremony, people milled around outside. After hanging around the area for a while, we decided it was time to head back to our hotel to have some fun.

AFTER MY DOCTORAL STUDIES

Living In The Moment

We got back to the hotel and changed our clothes. I changed out of my blinged out sneakers, t-shirt, and black pants I chose to wear instead of heavy jeans. I was grateful for what I wore beneath the robe because I had no idea the heaviness of a doctoral robe.

Since I was unfamiliar with the city, I did not know where we should go. I knew no one wanted to waste a gorgeous Saturday afternoon in this city. After taking a short rest, we decided to head out.

In 2014 when I visited this city for the second time, I researched this weird looking mountain. I read that people died from tumbling off of it. I decided if I ever returned to this city, I would like to go on the trail to see what it was like. I remembered the request I released in 2014 and suggested we should drive to the mountain. We saw multimillion-dollar homes. The view from that vantage point was gorgeous. I could only imagine what it looked like at night.

I thought we were on the wrong side of the mountain because there was no section that showed any trails. After searching the internet, we realized that we were a few miles away from the walking trails. I was not dressed to tackle any trail adventures. I had changed into jeans and some regular sneakers. I said we could go and look, but I was not going to walk. I would wait in the van until everyone came back if they wanted to go exploring. As we got closer to this mountain, it gave me the heebie-jeebies.

It was enormous with rocks that looked like multiple distorted faces. When I realized where I was, it did not appear as creepy.

This was the mountain I wanted to see. It looked different up close. We pulled into the parking area and got out of the van. I heard that mountain calling me by name. It was so beautiful. There was no way I could walk away from it. While I walked to the entrance for the trail with my son, I told him he would surely need his cane for this one. He could not sweep the ground with it, but he could tap it to find his footing. I did my best to describe what I saw to him.

When we got to a flat area, I asked him to touch the ground to "see" what it felt like and describe it to me. The rest of the children were so excited, they passed us. While my son felt an enormous boulder, his dad grabbed him by the arm and off they went. They ended up in front of everyone. We walked until I saw a small area with a shelter that veered off the trail to the right.

I wanted a respite from the ninety-eight-degree heat and to see what was down below. I thought my family would continue since they could not contain their excitement, but they followed me. When we were ready, we started walking again. Eventually, I ended up in the back. One person who traveled with us was a family friend. He had a bright-white-toothed huge smile. With his huge smile and his fronts glowing, he asked? "Are you okay?"

I said, "Yes, I'm okay." I straight up fibbed. I huffed, and I puffed with each step I took, and I was thirsty, hot, sweaty, sticky, and dusty; we had just started. My blind son was ahead with his father; there was no excuse for me. Besides that, I received the gift I put into the atmosphere four years prior. Even though I dressed in heavy jeans and sneakers, there was no way I would throw that gift away.

I attended my graduation, my family and a friend we loved surrounded me, I lived in the present moment, and there wasn't anywhere else in the world I wanted to be at that moment. The only thing that would have spoiled that moment was me tumbling off the mountain, and I had no intentions of doing that. Not only am I too vain to embarrass myself like that, but I would not want anyone to capture the moment and put it onto social media. I had no cool points left to lose.

After I told the person I was okay, I continued to move forward and enjoyed the view with each step one foot in front of the other. Periodically I stopped to gaze behind me to see how far I traveled along the trail. Everything around me clothed in sheer beauty excited me and pushed me to take the next step toward the top. On either side of this beautiful trail, rocks filled with shallow caves impressed me with their massiveness. To my awe, boulders stood in ways that looked as if like they could be pushed over and provided a splendid view to gaze upon Mother Nature.

There is no way to accurately describe this natural beauty. Everyone enjoyed this new adventure which reflected the true meaning of living in the moment. I relished in every millisecond on that mountain trail. I expressed gratitude as I continued.

While walking up the trail, a kind stranger asked if we had enough water. I told him we did not. We were visiting and came up here on a whim. He told us if we began to feel hot, or thirsty to head back. We were all past hot and thirsty.

My ex-husband had his cell phone in hand and checked for shade on some kind of app. We asked this kind stranger, how far the shaded area was from our current location. He pointed and informed us that it was not much farther. We thanked him for his kindness and continued.

With strong reluctance to go much further, I asked my ex-husband how far to the shady area. I thought we would have found it sooner and felt we should heed the warning given by that stranger. He said, "It is right around the corner."

I said, "Okay," and kept walking.

With a slight but sudden right turn, we came to a natural shade area created by an enormous boulder. We were able to look down on the valley at the breathtaking sight. We enjoyed the shade and took in the view as far as our eyes could see. I mentioned what we saw to my son so that he could enjoy the experience also.

Right before the turn, there was a plaque mounted on a stand. I went and read it. There was a picture of a young male professional hiker who walked off the trail and fell to his death. We thought we were close to the top. Nothing could have been further from the truth. The sign showed how far we had made it up the trail --1,650 feet, and how high the summit was -- 2,100 feet. There was a warning to stop at this point if anyone could not tackle the more difficult half of the mountain. The message was a sure sign for us to stop and turn around. It was an easier trek down the mountain for four of us. One person quickly made the trek down. Three of us decided to choose our steps without rushing.

When we got to our vehicle we had to wait for my son and his dad. Though the trek going up was a little tricky, coming down was difficult. Some terrain was rockier than other parts and walking down was slower for my son. His dad held his arm the entire time often sliding as they carefully descended.

After we got to the car, the only thing we wanted to do was find somewhere to eat and drink. We found a franchise restaurant we were familiar with its name. I ordered the largest cup of lemonade they had. After everyone had eaten and rested, we drove across the street to a gift shop. Even though I do not drink, I love collecting shot glasses. I vowed not to leave the state without a specific one.

I went into this cluttered, eclectic shop and asked the owner if he had the shot glass that I wanted to obtain for my collection. After taking a few minutes to look through the entire display, I found the perfect silver and red shot glass. I also purchased cactus candy a regional gummy. After paying for my items and sharing the candy, we headed back to the hotel. We changed from our dusty clothing, took showers, and packed for our trip home.

Going Home

The next day was another early morning for us all. My trek up the mountain did the trick for my sleep as I slept like a baby and was refreshed the next morning. It was the best night's rest I had since I had gotten to the hotel.

After checking and rechecking to make sure we packed everything, we checked out of the hotel. We had no time to stop and eat. We returned our vehicle and caught a shuttle to the airport. When we arrived at the airport, it was like time sped up and then slowed down. The area was so overcrowded that an attendant sent us to curbside check-in. Going through security did not take long; so, we finally had time to stop and buy something to eat. My daughter and I went to purchase food for everyone. I wanted some orange juice, but the line at the coffee shop was too long and I dared not leave it to go looking for it.

Since I was able to board early with my son, I saved seats so we could all sit together. I put my son next to the window so he could have this new experience. After telling him all I could see were clouds since we were too high to see any houses, the flight attendant came by for drink service. I do not know what anyone else asked for, but my son and I asked for our trusted orange juice.

Going Home

The flight to our hometown was a dream. I was so engrossed in a movie which my ex-husband pulled up on his phone that I paid no attention to the time. Before I knew it, we were preparing for landing. After the flight, we had an hour drive back to my cozy home. Once back in our city our party of six separated; three of us went one way and the other three went their way. And, that ladies and gentlemen, is the end of our wonderful trip.

The next day, I looked for pictures of the second half of the mountain. I wanted to see what I may have missed. We made the correct decision to turn around. Getting on the trail could be scratched off my bucket list with making it to the summit replacing it. We all want to return one day and trek to the summit. Next time we will be better prepared to conquer it.

I viewed the video of my graduation ceremony. To my surprise, during the time the commencement speaker gave his speech, the university showed advertisements and a countdown clock instead. I was looking forward to this speech, but it was not meant to be.

I spent the day returning phone calls to friends and family. My sister informed me the university advertised so much she wanted to enroll. It was a joke, but it was the very thing I wanted nothing to do with. Friends and family were not happy with having to wait for the ceremony to start, but they were excited to see me walk the stage and hooded. I remembered a moment before the graduation ceremony when I stood in line to take my picture. A man walked up the line and asked, "Was your process hell?"

Everyone said, "Yes!"

As for me, I said, "It was beyond hell."

It was his way to ascertain that it was not just him. One lady said she was so happy to be there because she did not think she would ever finish. No one went into detail about their unpleasant experiences and it revealed that no one graduated in the time-frame in which the university promised or advertised. None of us came out unscathed, but we did come out with Dr. in front of our names.

If there was anyone who graduated in three years, I did not meet them. Regardless, it did not matter that day. At the end of our journey, we were all equal, we all sat in the same section in front of everyone, we all wore our robes and crowns and we were hooded. We were not concerned about the hell, anymore.

We focused on the fact we were there, and we made it. None of the other stuff mattered anymore.

Reflections

There is a reason the rear window on your bus is smaller than your front window. Some people say you should never look back, but I believe we should look back for a brief moment from time to time. It is wonderful to look back and reflect on where you came from. It makes the end of the journey so much sweeter in the end and it keeps you humble.

As you drive, your rear view will become smaller until it gradually disappears. Your front view will become bigger until you arrive at your destination. Past and present work together and you cannot avoid either. Even if you stop driving your bus, you will eventually end up in the past.

In my moment of reflection and looking through my rear window, I saw many mistakes I made during my journey. Some were my fault due to my lack of knowledge while much can be attributed to the university's policies, procedures, and committee chairs. Because of these, I crammed three years into six years of hell.

I neither took the time to thoroughly research this university nor did I thoroughly research the university I attended for those expensive short twelve weeks. I went to the other university because someone I

So, You Want To Be A Doctoral Learner Huh? ARE YOU NUTS?!

knew was attending which was the wrong reason to choose any higher education program. My friend started her program at least two years before I started mine and did not defend her dissertation until eight months after I defended mine. Her program was also advertised as a three-year program.

If you find a program that advertises you can earn your Ph.D. or doctorate in two or three years, seize those as red flags. It is very possible to graduate in three years, but for that to happen everything must fall into perfect alignment. In many cases, it will not. Also, investigate how long their program has been in existence, and if it is less than five years, run. Okay, I will say it again, run! run!

I listened to counselors who told me the sunny side, but not the whole side. Some things I could not have known until I was too deep in the program. A program that started with five figures, compounded into six figures. I paid for travel and lodging during residencies. I had to come out-of-pocket close to $8,000 dollars to finish my program. That odyssey is another book. Had I known then, what I know now, I would not have chosen this university. Please trust me when I say the difficult program was not the issue; all programs will be difficult. The way the university treated learners and did not share the entire truth was my issue as it has been for others too.

Many unaccounted complications arose such as my university constantly changing the program requirements while learners were going through it. It was often explained as an attempt to make the program better. However, it made the program longer and my cohort group should have been grandfathered in under the guidelines in which we joined the program. I am grateful I completed my program, but I am not sure the emotional and financial devastation was worth it. In a year, I will be able to answer that question with certainty.

I implore you to research the type of accreditation your university received and what agency granted it. Ask about graduation rates and read student reviews and their experiences from start to graduation. Find out how much the entire program costs, then add the cost of your textbooks, supplies, travel needs and graduation assessments to that. Investigate the number of credits hours you will earn per course and how many credits you need to graduate. These things are important.

Ideally, depending on your program, the more credits granted per course, the shorter the program. The shorter the program, the less it should cost you to finish; and that depends on the cost for each credit hour. Factor in $5,000 dollars for research items and residencies if you must attend. Ask if there are any extended courses. A university will never tell you this information up front. Ask how much each extended course will cost and inquire if you would have to pay out-of-pocket.

I also suggest no matter your circumstance do not lose your temper; use your anger to motivate you. I understand if you do; I get it, but anger takes an emotional toll on you and it is not worth it in the end. I did not like the hatred I felt toward my second chairperson. I did not like how it made me feel. It hurt me more than it ever hurt him. He did not care about me or my feelings. The only thing I wanted, was to get away from him. Under the circumstances, he should have been moved. Every course I took with him caused me to go deeper and deeper into debt. The university was a co-conspirator, and I felt like I was robbed in the process. Before I enrolled in a new class, the university finance department made me supply some form of payment which had to be kept on file. If I did not contact them, rest assured they contacted me with the vengeance of a bill collector.

As awful as this may appear, I said if I did not graduate, I would return to the brick and mortar university and pluck every brick out of those buildings one by one for each dollar of debt I owed. The silliest part? I meant it although I knew I could not do it. At the minimum, it was great to just think it, and recognize my true feelings. Get ready, at some point in your journey you will remember this and say, "Me too!" We all do.

Here is a piece of advice; make bonds with other supportive learners so you can help each other as this is one journey you will not be able to travel alone, and you should not. Some of your friendships will become meaningful as you progress through the program while others will be less supportive.

A learner during my first residency conducted a poll to determine how many of their cohorts and doctoral students planned to attend their graduation. Many said they did not want to spend the money after going into debt paying for the program. One thing I was certain of was I knew to obtain my doctorate required a lot of demanding work and my graduation and being hooded would be my reward. Remember, years later I was so full of bitterness I initially refused to go to my own graduation.

I added my graduation trip not only for myself but also for my family as they meant everything to me and especially for you. Please recognize from the start that your family is a part of your doctoral journey and they sacrifice much for you as you complete your degree. They are aware of the moments you could not join in a family activity or when you wrote into the wee hours of the night and forgot to tuck them in or when you were simply exhausted and needed five minutes alone. They do not harness ill will as they recognize your goal and triumphed with your accomplishment. Therefore, I encourage everyone to go to your graduation and celebrate this milestone. There will never be another milestone like it, ever! If you can take the family, do it. It took me almost six years to strut those short steps, and it was wonderful. You deserve to wear your royal robe. You deserve to be crowned. You deserve to be hooded. You deserve to have your name announced into the atmosphere like the king or queen that you are. You earned it!

If you cannot afford to fly, go to an online store, and buy a cheap graduation tam, robe, and hood. Have graduation at home and have pictures taken. Do not allow bitterness to deprive you of what you earned. If you are not interested in buying your regalia, do something special with your family.

While going through your program, say thank you and say it a lot. Say it every time your committee members help you. Say it when you write your acknowledgment letter. Thank you opens invisible doors. Thank you opened a door for me when I decided to close it.

You are not your committee member's only learner. No one knows how many times a day they may have gotten an angry email they did not deserve. They are human and may have the same stressors that you and I do. Sometimes they need to know how much they are appreciated.

There is nothing in this world I could do or say to show my professors, chairperson, committee members, and my reviewer how much I appreciate them. I went through hell, but it worked out. For many, it did not and for many, it will not. All around me learners left. I thought I was being foolish for staying.

I was verbally assaulted by a male cohort member who I held in high regard. If you were sad, and he started laughing, you could not help but laugh too. He spoke about the university with vitriol. I understood his anger. I threw him out of our group because he made inflammatory, negative, and hurtful comments. He became angrier when I would not drop out of the program after he did.

I asked him if the way he wrote his messages to me was the manner in which he wrote in class because it looked like he typed his message with his toes. He was livid! He called me disrespectful, and a "Willie Lynch." I never heard the name before so as a true researcher I looked it up.

I was incensed by this disrespect and asked him to never speak to me again. He must have seen my name somewhere, and that I received my doctorate because he wrote to congratulate me and asked me to work on something with him. I declined the offer, I forgave him and wished him the best.

I could not tell anyone when I would finish my program. I got tired of people asking me when I was going to graduate. FYI never ask a learner that question. I started telling them as soon as I find out, I would let them know.

Many learners leave because of personality clashes with their committee members, the university's unwillingness to allow committee member changes, running out of funds, being stressed out, health issues, marital issues, death, and much more. If you find the journey too difficult, then it is okay to quit. Keep in mind, both quitting and finishing are forever; you decide. Make sure whatever decision you make is one you can remain in a place of peace.

Conclusion

Earning an advanced degree does not discriminate or show bigotry. No matter what your class, your gender, your ethnicity, your race, your creed, your cultural differences, or your orientation, the process is going to leave you bruised and battered. As you drive your bus, you will go through the mountains and valleys. Some roads will be bumpy, others will be smooth, while some will have huge potholes that you will not be able to get out of or to avoid.

No matter the outcome when you get to the end of your road you are never going to be the same. You will either be bitter or better. It is up to you to choose which one. I came out extremely bitter. Bitterness is what made me start this book, but better allowed me to finish it. Try as hard as you can to enjoy the journey by finding the joy inside of your trials as you progress through it. The words thank you became the joy inside my trials. They changed my life forever.

I wish I had enjoyed the process more. I was trying so hard to figure out how I would get through it, I could not breathe enough to enjoy my trip until I was close to the end. I walked around with a dark cloud over my head for so long it eventually started to rain. I did not think the rain would ever stop, but it did, and the sun came out.

Conclusion

The committee member who did not help me did not help anyone else. Not one learner succeeded under him. He resigned after three years. The university was complicit in what this professor was doing. They should be held liable and reimburse every dime used while learners were in his courses. No one has any idea of the emotional and financial devastation this one individual caused learners. Bringing it up would be a waste of time because I know what I would be up against.

I came a long way from hating him to wishing him the best. There is never a reason to wish bad on another person even if they wish it on you. The law or reciprocity will take care of everything and the best revenge is a successful life.

I hated my university so much I prayed the program would shut down. I just wanted to get out before it did. One day when I was in a place of peace and enlightenment, I thought of the professors who were good to me over the years, the counselors, librarians, tech support, my committee members, my cohort members, my friends, and the learners who were in the middle of the program. I thought of all the people who depended on their jobs to put food on their tables and pay their bills.

If my prayer was answered, what would happen to the innocent people who lost their livelihood? What would happen to learners who would have to walk away with nothing except loan repayments? I changed my prayer. I prayed for the program to stop accepting new learners until it was restructured. Only one prayer got answered. The only one I should have been praying for all along; me becoming Dr. Davis.

When you see your name on your diploma, when you see your study on the world wide web when you get a notification that someone read your study, when you see your name as a citation in someone else's study and when you hear people call you doctor none of the bad experiences will matter. You will have scars; but if you focus on the end results, they will not bother you as much.

It has been a few months since graduation, and I am still trying to adjust. For some reason, it has not settled in my soul and I am doing my best to find my footing. I am still "Mom" and I am trying to adjust to friends and family calling me Dr. Davis. Sometimes when someone calls me Dr. Davis, professionally, I have to remind myself they are talking to me. When I remember that I am the one they are calling Dr. Davis, it feels lovely. It really does!

What will I do with my degree now? I am leaving all the opportunities open to see where my new adventure takes me. I am always waiting for that next daredevil opportunity. I do know that I can never sit behind anyone's desk for eight hours a day again. Now, I sit behind my own to help other learners to cross their finish line. I made a vow that if I ever owned my own company with employees, I will have a clause written in, to allow employees to get up every two hours and walk around for ten minutes. Maybe there is research potential in that idea.

After reading and re-reading this manuscript, I was reminded of how depressed I was for so long. Upon reflecting on the incredible financial difficulties, I endured for three years, the tears I shed, the emotional roller-coaster I was on, and how my life could have been snuffed out, I am grateful I am still here on this earth. I went through a week of sadness and wondered if I should publish this book. It brought back a lot of emotions and the things I had forgotten. Though there were more bad than good, the good was wonderful and I focused on that.

After continuing with my everyday life, I realized this book had to be published. I went through what I did so you would not have too. It is an obligation I must see all the way to the end. I want no more incomplete projects in my life.

I relive my story every time I get a learner who is unable to progress. I feel so bad for them because I understand. I do my best to show compassion and try to assure them that everything will work out. I feel like a counselor sometimes as I talk them through the hopelessness. I share my story and let them know that everything will work out and everything has value. They must also understand, they must work hard.

The last time I cried was tears of triumph at my graduation. Those are the only tears you should shed. When you get through this process, you will be transformed from a caterpillar into a beautiful butterfly.

Conclusion

Everything about you will transform. The way you think will change, the way you walk will change, the way you speak will change, and the way you act will change.

I am less tolerant of foolishness from people, and I do not stress over things as much as I used too. I keep negative people, and negative energy away from me as much as possible. If someone decides they no longer want to be in my life whether friendship or relationship, I release them with full blessings. I understand that whatever their purpose may have been in my life was fulfilled. I do not chew on every detail trying to figure out what went wrong.

I have always been an exceedingly kind and compassionate woman, but I purpose to become better. I love more, and I love for no reason. I express it more in the things that I do, and the things that I say. I am not perfect, and I do not always get it right. I accepted years ago that I am flawed. If I were perfect, God could never use me. I am humble enough to apologize when I slight someone. There is much freedom in that.

When I chose to start this journey, I had no idea why I made the choice. What I do know is the purpose of this journey was bigger than me, and it is bigger than you. If you want those three letters because you want the title, or you like the way the letters look next to your name, then you have no business in a program like this.

When this process gets finished beating you down to the lowest level of humility, it is there you will realize that this journey is not about you. It is about those participants out there. It is about making a difference in the lives of others who need your voice. The rewards you get are three letters before your name and a legacy for your family. If learners remember this, it will put all the heartache into perspective and allow them to keep their eyes on the road.

Do not worry about the letters, they are coming. Focus on your assignments and correct those mistakes your committee members tell you to fix two thousand times. Get your research completed and let everything else fall into place. If you do everything you are supposed to, the natural order of things will make everything work out in your favor. I am telling you this from my experience.

No matter how insignificant you feel your study is, it will help someone. One of my reviewers told me my dissertation was more like a book report. I was deeply offended because I knew my design choice was the right one.

He had no idea how hard I had to struggle to pay for each class, how far I drove to collect my data, how broke I was as I collected and analyzed my data, how painful it was to sit and listen to those stories, or how my participants trusted me to come into their homes while they were alone.

They could not see what I looked like, they did not know if I would hurt them or not, and they had never met me before; yet, they trusted me. The only thing that mattered to them was that the study needed to be done.

The university personnel who looked past me when I pleaded for help and my chairperson were roadblocks put in my way to keep me from getting to the finish line. My ability to drive my bus got me to my destination, but I did not get there alone.

God was my navigator, my committee members, my wonderful professors, reviewers, librarians, technical support workers, counselors, and editors were my road guards. My participants, friends, and family sat in those seats and cheered me on when I wanted to stop driving.

While going through your doctoral program, things will happen that will make you question the universe. It will make you question yourself, make you question God, and it will make you question your sanity. If you do not believe me, search the internet, and do research on stress for Ph.D. or doctoral learners. That "sheepskin" you earn is not worth losing any part of yourself. Get on that bus, strap yourself in, check your mirrors and enjoy the gorgeous view as you drive your bus.

In this book, I gave you information on some of my experiences during my doctoral journey and tips to help you avoid the potholes. You will have your own bumps during your journey that you will have to navigate. Some of you will drive into a pothole and not be able to get out. For those of you who do, hold the steering wheel as tight as you can and take control of your bus.

Conclusion

To all my cohorts who are still in their program, to all of you courageous, tenacious, and wonderful learners who I may never meet, I parked my bus on the other side of the finish line. I am waiting for you to cross it. I will not leave until you do. Look for me; I will be the short one with the loudest voice and the biggest smile.

I hope you enjoyed the bus ride as much as I enjoyed having you with me. I hope you found a nugget of wisdom that will help you on your journey. Always remain positive and humble. If you decide to become a professor or committee member, please remember what it was like when you were going through your journey. Temper your responses to your learners with mercy and compassion. For those of you who are having a challenging time with your program, I will say this to you. If you can hang in there and see it for what it is, you will be fine. If you choose to walk away because it proves too difficult to continue no matter the reason, you will be fine. Whatever decision you make, know that you are not nuts!

Research Assignments

To get you on your way to becoming an outstanding researcher, below are terms you might use in your journey. Use your research skills to learn more about each term. Although they might look difficult at the moment, you will become familiar with several of these terms. Include citations within the last three to five years and have fun!

All but Dissertation (ABD)
Attrition
Conceptual framework
Case Study
Cohort
Compare
Contrast
Correlational
Deductive reasoning
Dependent Variable
Descriptive
Design
Doctor of Education (Ed. D)
Educational Specialist (EDS)
Empirical Article
Experimental
Ethnography
Grounded theory
Hand coding
Hypothesis
Iteration
Independent variable
Inductive reasoning

Institutional Review Board (IRB)
Literature Review
Methodology
Mixed Methods
Narrative
Population
Peer-reviewed
Doctor of Philosophy (Ph.D.)
Phenomenological
Problem Statement
Purpose Statement
Qualitative
Quantitative
Quasi-experimental
Sample
Seminal Article
Scholarly
Substantive
Synthesizing
Thematic analysis
Theoretical foundation

Research Assignments

What are the five main chapters of your dissertation?

1. _____

2. _____

3. _____

4. _____

5. _____

What is the difference between qualitative, quantitative, and mixed methods research?

Investigate empirical research articles and identify the need for further research that may be of interest to you.

Matching Exercise

Use these terms and put them under the correct methodology and design.

Action research, Case Study, Concurrent Nested, Concurrent Triangulation, Concurrent Transformative, Correlational, Descriptive, Correlational, Ethnography, G*Power, Grounded theory, Mixed Methods Narrative, Phenomenological, Qualitative, Quantitative, Quasi-experimental, Sequential Explanatory, Sequential Exploratory, Sequential Transformative.

Mixed Methods Methodology

Mixed Methods Designs

Qualitative Methodology

Qualitative Designs

Quantitative Methodology

Quantitative Designs

Website Resources

Here are websites that I and other learners used to help us succeed. As you continue your program, you will find others that will help you.

https://www.researchgate.net/ (Scholarly Articles)
https://www.wikipedia.org/ (Articles and Book References)
https://transcribe.wreally.com/ (Transcription Program)
https://www.thumbtack.com/ (Transcription Services)
https://www.refworks.com/ (Reference Builder)
https://reciteworks.com/ (Citation and Reference Checker)
https://scholar.google.com/ (Scholarly Articles and Books)
https://www.mendeley.com/ (Reference Manager)
http://www.litassist.com/ (Literature Review Assistance)
https://statistics.laerd.com/ (Quant Data Analysis)
https://www.qsrinternational.com/ (Qual and Mix Data Analysis)
https://www.livescribe.com/en-us/ (Data Collection Recorder)
https://www.youtube.com/ (Tutoring/Codebook)
http://www.apastyle.org/index.aspx (APA Formatting)
https://www.randomizer.org/ (Use for Random Sampling You Choose)
http://www.hemingwayapp.com/ (Grade Level Writing)
https://books.google.com/ (Books for Researchers)

So, You Want To Be A Doctoral Learner Huh? ARE YOU NUTS?!

Visualization Graphics

Congratulations Dr._____**You did it!**

So, You Want To Be A Doctoral Learner Huh? ARE YOU NUTS?!

Congratulations Dr._____**You did it!**

NOTES

INDEX

"empirical" article, 10
"What if" tips, 34
academia, 10
affirmations, 41
aligned, 14, 18, 19, 22, 58
Aligning, 22
Alignment, 22, See aligning
all but dissertation, 17
American Psychological Association, 23
APA, 23, 28, 29, 30, 119
APA manual, 29
attrition, 3, 83
audio recording, 81
BODY, 37
body of literature, 9, 11
body of the dissertation, 13
codebook, 87
cohorts, 14, 114
commencement, 95, 103
comparing and contrasting, 24
conceptual framework, 13, 25, 26
conclusion, 20, 21
conducting research, 19
conferred, 96
cope with my frustration, 33
credit hours, 6, 11
cross-referencing, 25
curriculum-based, 9
Data analysis, 13
data analysis program, 18, 86, 87
decline to answer, 78
demographic questionnaire, 76
discussion, 6, 19, 20, 21, 47, 48, 82
dissertation committee, 14, 22
Doctor of Education (D.Ed. or Ed.D.), 9
Doctor of Education degree, 8
Doctor of Philosophy (Ph.D.), 3, 9, 116
doctoral journey, v, 1, 5, 35, 42, 51, 114, 127
doctoral lingo, 12
double-edge sword, 10, 14
failure, 3, 6, 73
field-testing, 76
filename, 27
final defense, 90
final gap statement. See gap
first stage
body of a dissertation. See body of a dissertation
fourth stage
body of a dissertation. See body of a dissertation
gap, 14, 19, 20, 21, 22, 24, 58, 60, 78, 86
GPA, 18, 46
grade point average, 18
graduation robes. See regalia
hood, 95, 108
hypothesis, 13, 14, 21
Institutional Review Board, 52, 78, 116

Index

instruments, 10, 14, 76, 77, 84
in-text citation, 26
IRB, 52, 78, 83, 84, 116
Lack of available research, 25
letter of confidentiality, 85
Library of Congress, 2, 31
limitation, 82
limitations, 21
literature review, 13, 23, 24, 28, 30
logic, 77, 78
mantra, 41
methodologist, 18, 48, 49, 50, 54, 58, 60, 72, 74
methodology, 13, 14, 28, 29, 118
MIND, 33
mixed methods methodology, 14
mock interview, 78
need statement, 14, 19, 20, 21, 22, 58
peer reviewed, 10
Ph.D. program, 6
phenomenological, 13
population, 23
problem statement, 13
purpose statement, 13, 21, 25, 86
qualitative methodology, 14
quantitative methodology, 14
questionnaires, 29
recommendations for future research, 21
regalia, 40, 93, 95, 96, 108
reliability, 29
replicated study, 20
research questions, 14, 21, 25, 78, 86
residency, 12, 15, 16, 18, 19, 20, 22, 35, 56, 58, 59, 60, 93, 108
responsibility as a learner, 14
riding the coattails, 9
save your document, 26, 27
second stage
body of a dissertation. See body of a dissertation
secondary resources, 25
skills to become a fine-tuned researcher, 21
sleep, 35, 36, 37, 56, 69, 70
SPIRIT, 39
statistics, 6, 8, 18, 119
stress, 1, 23, 30, 34, 35, 37, 40, 41, 58, 61, 64, 65, 70, 78, 112, 114
stressors, 33, 109
study group, 35
tam, 95, 108
theoretical foundation, 13, 25
third stage
body of a dissertation. See body of a dissertation
time stamp, 26, 27
tip, 28, 29, 62
transcriptionist, 82, 85, 86
validity, 29
variables, 13
visualization, 39
websites, 21, 25, 85, 86, 119
writer's block, 34

ABOUT THE AUTHOR

Dr. L. A. Davis was born on the trade-winds-kissed island of St. Thomas, United States Virgin Islands and is a proud member of Zeta Phi Beta Sorority Incorporated. She completed her Ed.D. in 2017. During her doctoral journey, she encountered many obstacles that prompted her to write her first book. She founded The Dissertation Café to coach doctoral learners.

https://thedissertationcafe.com

Contact Information

Dr. L. A. Davis
2403 W Stan Schlueter Loop #690923
Killeen, Texas 76549
Davislad2018@gmail.com

www.ingramcontent.com/pod-product-compliance
Lightning Source LLC
LaVergne TN
LVHW041639060526
838200LV00040B/1640